MEMOIRS
OF THE
ASIATIC SOCIETY OF BENGAL

VOL. V. No. 3, PP. 43—113

THE PALAS OF BENGAL

MEMOIRS
OF THE
ASIATIC SOCIETY OF BENGAL
VOL. V. No. 3, PP. 43—113

THE PALAS OF BENGAL

BY

R. D. BANERJI,
M.A., Indian Museum, Calcutta.

GYAN

Published by

GYAN

Gyan Publishing House
5, Ansari Road
Daryaganj, New Delhi-110002
Phone: 011-47034999, 9811692060
E-mail: books@gyanbooks.com

Distribution Network
gyanbooks.com
India, USA, Canada, UK, Australia, France

ISBN : 978-81-212-2842-8 (HB)
First Published, 1915

2nd Impression 2021

Printed at: Gyan Press, Delhi.

The Palas of Bengal
Author: R. D. Banerji

MEMOIRS

OF THE

ASIATIC SOCIETY OF BENGAL

VOL. V, No. 3, pp. 43—113.

THE PĀLAS OF BENGAL.

BY

R. D. BANERJI, M.A., *Indian Museum, Calcutta.*

CALCUTTA:

PRINTED AT THE BAPTIST MISSION PRESS, AND PUBLISHED BY

THE ASIATIC SOCIETY, 1, PARK STREET.

1915.

20-8-15.

PREFACE.

The ground plan of a history of Eastern India from 800 to 1200 A.D. has already been sketched out by Mahāmahopādhyāya Hara Prasād Sāstrī in his short introduction to Sandhyākaranandi's *Rāmacarita*. At that time I intended to develop it and add all the available material in a fresh article. This article was finished in October 1911. It was revised by Dr. J. Ph. Vogel, Ph.D., then Officiating Director General of Archaeology, and submitted to the Society. For various reasons, the publication of this part of the Memoirs has been delayed, among which may be mentioned the loss of several impressions of inscriptions.

I have not been able to edit the inscriptions quoted in the body of this paper to my satisfaction, on account of want of time and space. The readings quoted are for the most part true readings. Pandit Binod Bihari Bidyabinod has helped me considerably in deciphering them. The majority of the new records were read by him, and the texts were then revised and modified by me. But in each case a mechanical estampage has been reproduced so that a worthier scholar may re-edit it from the plates. The historical information supplied by each record has been given in the form of a summary in the body of the text.

I am indebted to Mahāmahopādhyāya Hara Prasād Sāstrī, C.I.E., Dr. J. Ph. Vogel, Ph.D., Dr. D. B. Spooner, B.A., Ph.D., Prof. Jadu Nath Sarkar and Mr. K. P Jayaswal. B.A., Bar.-at-Law, for many suggestions. To my friend Mr. Surendra Nath Kumar of the Imperial Library, Calcutta, I am indebted for translations of various passages in French or German. Dr. F. W Thomas, Ph.D., of the India Office Library, and Dr. A. F R. Hoernle kindly obtained for me photographs of the historical colophones of manuscripts preserved in the Bodleian or the Royal Asiatic Society's Library. Dr. Thomas obtained for me two impressions of votive inscriptions of Mahendrapāla in the British Museum. Mr. G. H. Tipper, M.A., F.G.S., then Honorary General Secretary of the Society, very kindly obtained photographs of the historical colophones of manuscripts preserved in the Cambridge University's Library and the Bengal Asiatic Society's collections. In fact, without his aid it would have been quite impossible for me to complete this work.

INDIAN MUSEUM,
Calcutta, the 30th May, 1914.

The Pālas of Bengal.

By R. D. BANERJI, M.A., *Indian Museum, Calcutta.*

[With Plates XXIV—XXXII, XXXVI—XXXVIII.]

CHAPTER I.

INTRODUCTION.

After the death of Harṣavarddhana, nothing is definitely known about the history of Bengal and Bihar, till the rise of the Pālas. In fact the only definite date after the death of Harṣavarddhana, is the year 66, of the Harṣa era, on the Shāhpur image of Sūryya.[1] We know from the Aphsaḍ inscription of Ādityasena, that Mādhavagupta was the contemporary of Harṣa,[2] and that Ādityasena succeeded in making himself independent in Magadha. The Deo-Banārak inscription of Jīvitagupta II carries the genealogy of the family for three generations further. These princes Devagupta, Viṣṇugupta and Jīvitagupta II continued to assume Imperial titles, though most probably their possessions were insignificant. The dynasty came to an end with the last-named prince, Jīvitagupta II.

The Guptas of Magadha.

The exact circumstances which led to the fall of this ancient dynasty are not known, but it seems certain that the event took place in troublesome times. Bengal was run over by Yaśovarmmadeva of Kanauj during the first two decades of the eighth century A.D.[3] Most probably Jīvitagupta II was the king who was overthrown by this invasion. Ādityasena's only definite date is 671 A.D., and this gives us about 40 or 50 years for four generations, which is certainly not too much. We do not know anything about the successors of Jīvitagupta II, but we know of several other foreign invasions of Bengal about the same time from contemporary records. The invasion from Kanauj was followed by one from Assam. The King Harṣadeva conquered Bengal, Orissa and the Northern Sarkars (*Gauḍ=Oḍr=ādi-Kaliṅga-Kośala-pati*). As his grandson, Jayadeva, the Licchavi, was reigning in the sixth decade of the eighth century A.D.,[4] the date of his maternal grandfather must be placed some time earlier. Most probably this invasion from Assam closely followed upon the heels of that from Kanauj, or we may one day be surprised to learn that both armies invaded Bengal jointly. Harṣadeva must have held Bengal for a sufficiently long time, so as to enable him to pass through that country and conquer *Oḍra* (Orissa) *Kaliṅga* (Northern Sarkars), and Kośala (Orissa Hill Tracts). The *Gauḍa-vaho* and the Rājataraṅginī has familiarized us with the

The dark period.

Foreign invasions.

---

[1] Fleet's Gupta Inscriptions, Vol. III, pp. 209-10.

[2] Ibid., p. 207.

[3] J.R.A.S., 1908, p. 76.

[4] Ind. Ant., Vol. IX, p. 178.

story of the banished king, Jayāpīḍa, who came to Bengal, married the daughter of the king, and freed him from the subjection of his liege-lord.[1] According to the able translator of the Rājataraṅginī, the true date of this king is between 760 and 800 A.D. Finally Bengal was conquered by the Gurjara and Rāṣṭrakūṭa kings. The Gurjara king Vatsarāja, according to the Gwalior inscription of Mihira-Bhoja, had seized by main force the imperial sway from the house of Bhaṇḍi:—

From Kanauj, Assam.

Khyātād=Bhaṇḍi-kulān=madotkaṭa-kari-prākāra durllaṅghato yaḥ sāmrājyam=adhijya-kārmmuka-sakhā saṁkhye haṭhād=agrahīt—*verse* 7.[2]

Most probably after the fall of Harṣavarddhana, the family of his cousin Bhaṇḍi succeeded to the Empire. Bhaṇḍi is mentioned in the *Harṣacarita* as the mother's brother's son of Harṣa.[3] Vatsarāja is said to have conquered Bengal very easily and taken away from its king the radiantly white royal umbrellas. In the Wani grant of the Rāṣṭrakūṭa king Govinda III, his father Dhruvarāja is said to have taken away these umbrellas from Vatsarāja and driven him away into the desert:—

Helā-svīkṛta-Gauḍa-rājya-kamalā-mattaṁ praveśy-acirād = durmārgam = marumadhyam=aprati-balair=yo Vatsarājaṁ balaiḥ Gauḍīyaṁ Śaradindupādadhavalaṁ chatradvayaṁ kevalaṁ tasmān = n = āhṛta tad-yaśo = pi kakubhaṁ prānte sthitaṁ tat-kṣaṇāt.

"Having with his armies, which no other army could withstand, quickly caused Vatsarāja, intoxicated with the goddess of the sovereignty of the country of Gauḍa, that he had acquired with ease, to enter upon the path of misfortune in the centre of the deserts or Maru, he took away from him not only the two royal umbrellas of Gauḍa, that were as radiantly white as the rays of the autumn moon, but almost, at the same moment, his fame that had reached to the extremities of the regions."[4]

The late Mr. A. M. T. Jackson supposed that the country conquered by Vatsarāja was Thanesar.[5] But the Gurjara king conquered Gauḍa and Vaṅga at the same time and the two umbrellas were, most probably, one for Gauḍa and the other for Vaṅga like the double crown of Egypt:—

Gauḍendra-Vaṅgapati nirjjaya-durvvidagdha sad=gurjjareśvara dig=arggalatāṁ ca yasya,

Nītvā bhujaṁ vihata-mālava-rakṣaṇārthaṁ svāmī tath=ānyam-api rājya-phalāni bhuṅkte.—Baroda plates of Karkarāja.[6]

The Radhanpur grant also contains the verse about the defeat of Vatsarāja by Dhruva.[7] So according to the Wani and Radhanpur grants Dhruva, father of the Rāṣṭrakūṭa king Govinda III, drove Vatsarāja back into the desert, and wrested from him the double royal umbrellas of Gauḍa, and according to the Baroda grant

1 Mem. A.S.B., Vol. III, p. 3, note 2.
2 Ann. Rep. Arch. Surv. Ind., 1903-04, p. 281.
3 Cowell and Thomas, *Harsacarita*, Or. Tr. Fund Series, p. 116.
4 Ind. Ant., Vol. XI, p. 157.
5 J.R.A.S., 1905, pp. 103-04.
6 Ind. Ant., Vol. XII, p. 160, ll. 39-40.
7 Epi. Ind., Vol. VI, p. 243.

Govinda III caused Karkarāja's arm to become the doorbar of the country of the Lord of the Gurjaras, who had become evilly inflamed by conquering the Lord of Gauḍa and Vaṅga. The verses in both grants do not refer to the same person. The first verse refers to Vatsarāja, the contemporary of Dhruva, but the second verse refers to Nāgabhaṭa II, son of Vatsarāja, who was defeated by Govinda III.

This brings us to the fourth foreign invasion of this period, the invasion of the Rāṣṭrakūṭas. It is evident from the verses quoted above that the Gurjara king's conquest was not a lasting one. Close on his heels followed the southerner and obliged him to relinquish his conquests and even forced him to retire into the desert country, his original home. When the double white umbrella was snatched away from Vatsarāja, the Kingdom of Gauḍa and Vaṅga must also have passed into the hands of the Rāṣṭrakūṭa conquerer. Nothing is known definitely about the close of the Rāṣṭrakūṭa occupation, but most probably it did not last long. As soon the Rāṣṭrakūṭa forces were withdrawn, the local princes must have re-asserted their authority.

During this period of foreign invasions and consequent anarchy and misrule, the old Royal dynasty must have come to an end, the harassed populace felt the necessity of a strong and able ruler. They held an election about the details of which we know nothing. As a result of this election Gopāladeva, the son of a successful soldier named Vapyaṭa, was elected king. In the Khalimpur grant of Dharmmapāla it is said that the people made him take the hand of fortune:—

The election of a king by the subjects

Mātsya-nyāyam-apohitum prakṛtibhir-lakṣmyāḥ karaṅ-grāhitaḥ Śrī-Gopāla iti kṣitīśa-śirasām cuḍāmaṇis-tat-sutaḥ, Yasy-ānukriyate sanātana-yaśo-rāsir-diśām-āśaye śvetimnā yadi paurṇṇamāsa-rajanī jyotsn-ātibhāra-śriyā.—verse 4.[1]

The composer of the Khalimpur inscription puts the cause of this election very nicely in the above verse: *Mātsya-nyāyam-apohitum*, "to escape from anarchy," as Mr. K. P. Jayaswal translates it.[2] That the danger of being swallowed up into the kingdom of a powerful neighbour, was not exaggerated, is amply evident from the foregoing account of the foreign invasions of Bengal during the dark period.

Nothing is known about the origin of this new line of kings, who continued to hold sway over Bihar or Bengal till the final conquest of the country by the Muhammadans. In the oldest inscription of this dynasty Dayitaviṣṇu, the grandfather of Gopāla I, is called the progenitor of this line of kings, and it was stated, that he was sanctified by all sorts of knowledge (*sarvva-vidyāvadātaḥ*).[3] Most probably the family was of such a humble origin that even the names of Dayitaviṣṇu's forefathers were not known in the time of his great-grandson. In later biographical works and inscriptions like the Rāmacarita of Sandhyākara-nandi and the Kamauli grant of Vaidyadeva, mythical accounts are given of the origin of the Pālas. The Kamauli grant mentions very distinctly that

The origin of the dynasty.

---

[1] Ibid., Vol. IV, p. 248.
[2] *Arthaśāstra of Cāṇakya.*
[3] J.A.S.B., 1894, p. 47, and Mem. A.S.B., Vol. III, p. 3.

the king Vigrahapāla III was born in the race of the Sun.[1] The Rāmacarita and the Bengali poem Dharmmamaṅgala of Ghanarāma give a different account altogether. This account is given very fully in the *Kaṇurpālā* of Ghanarāma's work, according to which the kings of the Pāla dynasty after Dharmmapāla were really the descendants of the Sea-god. This tradition is not very coherent as Mahamahopadhyaya Hara Prasada Sastri has shown. In the Rāmacarita, king Dharmmapāla is mentioned as "the light of the race of the Sea."[2] Thus the Rāmacarita corroborates the tradition embodied in Ghanarāma's work to some extent. It shows that the origin of the new line of kings was remembered by the people long after their accession and even after their fall. The descent from the Sea most probably indicates that the forefathers of this line of kings came from the Sea and in the absence of a plausible account of their ancestry became known as the children of the Sea-God.

[1] Ibid., Vol. II, p. 350.

[2] Mem. A.S.B., Vol., III, pp. 2-3 and 20.

CHAPTER II.

GOPĀLA I AND DHARMMAPĀLA.

Gopāla I was most probably an elderly man when he was called to the throne. Nothing is stated definitely about him or the events of his reign in any of the numerous Pāla inscriptions. In the Khalimpur grant of his son Dharmmapāla we find that he married Deddadevī, the daughter of the king of the Bhadra country.[1] The Bhadras have been variously placed in Middle, Eastern or Southern India in the Bṛhat Saṁhita.[2] The Mungir grant of Devapāladeva mentions him as the type of a well-conducted king.[3] In the rest of the copper-plates of the Pāla dynasty the verse quoted below is used about Gopala I:—

Jitvā yaḥ kāma-kārī-prabhavam = abhibhavaṁ śāśvatīṁ prāpa śāntiṁ,
Sa śrīmān lokanātho jayati Daśabalosnyaś = ca Gopāladevaḥ.

We find this verse in the Bhagalpur grant of Nārāyaṇapāla, Dinajpur grant of Mahīpāla I, Amgachi grant of Vigrahapāla III, and the Manahali grant of Madanapāla. No inscriptions of this king either on stone or on plates of copper have been discovered as yet, as has been stated by Mr. V. A. Smith.[4] According to Mr. V. A. Smith, Gopāla I was the king of Bengal, who was defeated by the Gurjara king Vatsarāja. But in my humble opinion the Gurjara and Rāṣṭrakūṭa invasions must have taken place before the accession of Gopāla I. In the next reign we find that the king of Bengal was acknowledged supreme by all kings of Northern India. Now Gopāla was elected king by the people of Bengal and his position consequently was not very strong within his own possessions. He was the son of a military adventurer, and he must have wanted a long and peaceful reign to consolidate his power. The Gurjara king Vatsarāja must also have reigned for a pretty long time as he is mentioned in a Jaina work, which we shall examine later on, to be the contemporary of a king who was overthrown by the son of Gopāla. Most probably Gopāla I had a shorter reign than Vatsarāja, who had overrun Bengal before the accession of the former, but lived long enough to see the former's son conquer his former possessions.

Length of reign and successor.

According to Tārānātha, Gopāladeva is said to have reigned for 45 years and Mr. V. A. Smith puts accession to the year 732 A.D.,[5] but as we shall see later on when we come to the first definite date of this dynasty, that this is a little premature. Gopāladeva ascended the throne about 750 A.D. and was most probably succeeded by his son Dharmmapāladeva after a very short reign.

---

[1] Epi. Ind., Vol. IV, p. 248, v. 5. [2] Ind. Ant, Vol. XXII, pp. 174—5. [3] Ibid., Vol. XXI, p. 255. [4] Ibid. Vol. XXXVIII, p. 245. [5] J.R.A.S., 1909, p. 76.

Dharmmapāladeva, the second king of the Pāla dynasty, was the real founder of the greatness of his line and the Empire over which his successors ruled. He was also the leading figure in Northern Indian politics in the last half of the eighth and the first half of the ninth centuries A.D. Most probably Bengal enjoyed some respite from foreign invasions during the reign of Gopāla I, and after him, his son felt strong enough to take part in the disputes of the contemporary monarchs of Northern India, and to conduct long campaigns. Before proceeding to discuss the events of his reign we should consider his date which is the first fixed point in the History of Bengal during this period. The chronology of the Pālas of Bengal was for a long time in a hopelessly confused state. Leaving aside the earlier theories about the dates of the Pālas we find even in recent times widely divergent theories about the date of Dharmmapāla. In the XVth Volume of his reports the late Sir Alexander Cunningham fixed the date of Dharmmapāla's accession in 831 A.D. In his article[1] on the Cambay plates of Govinda III, Mr. D. R. Bhandarkar places Dharmmapāla in the earlier part of the tenth century.[2] Dharmmapāla's date seems to have become fixed from synchronisms, which have been given for the first time in the preface of the Rāmacarita of Sandhyākaranandi by the learned Editor. The synchronisms have also been noticed almost simultaneously by two other scholars—Mr. V. A. Smith[3] and Mr. D. R. Bhandarkar.[4]

Dharmmapāla.

The first question about the true date of Dharmmapāla was raised incidentally in 1891 by the late Dr. Kielhorn on a passage in the Bhagalpur grant of Nārāyaṇapala:—

Jitv = endra-rāja-prabhṛtīn = arātīn = upārjjitā yena Mahodaya Śrīḥ, dattaḥ punaḥ sa valin = ārthayitre Cakrayudhāy = ānativāmanāya.[5]

At that time Dr. Kielhorn was unable to identify the kings Indrarāja or Cakrāyudha. The discovery of the Khalimpur grant supplied some additional facts and the well-known verse :—

Bhojair-Matsaiḥ sa-Madraiḥ Kuru-Yadu-Yavan = Āvantī-Gandhāra-Kīrair = bhupair = vyālola-mauli-praṇati-pariṇataiḥ sādhu saṅgīryamānaḥ,
Hṛṣyat Pañcāla-vṛddh-oddhṛta-kanakamaya-svābhiṣekodakumbho dattaḥ śrī-Kānyakubjas = sa-lalita-calita-bhrulatā-lakṣma-yena.[6]

For a long time nothing could be made out of the historical allusions in the two verses quoted above. It was known to the scholars that a certain verse of the Jaina Hari-vaṁśa-purāṇa referred to a king named Indrarāja who was a contemporary of Vatsarāja and was living in the year 705 of the Śaka era, i.e. 783 A.D.[7] But so far nobody was able to connect Indrāyudha with the Indrarāja of the Bhagalpur grant. Some time before November 1896, a stone inscription was discovered in some excavations which were being carried

1 Arch. Survey Rep., Vol. XV, p. 150.
2 Epi. Ind., Vol. VII, p. 33.
3 J.R.A.S., 1908, p. 252.
4 Epi. Ind., Vol. IX, p. 26, note 4.
5 Ind. Ant., Vol. XX, pp. 187-88.
6 Epi. Ind., Vol. IV, p. 248.
7 Ind. Ant., Vol. XV, p. 141, Peterson's 4th report on the search of Skt. MSS. in the Bombay Presidency.

on near the city of Gwalior, and a pencil rubbing of which with a photograph was handed over to the late Dr. Kielhorn by Dr. A. F. R. Hœrnle. A summary of this inscription was published by Dr. Kielhorn and it became known that Nāgabhaṭa II, son of Vatsarāja of the Gurjara-Pratīhāra family, conquered a king named Cakrāyudha, "whose low state was manifested by his dependence on another (or others)," and defeated the Lord of Vaṅga.[1] The Cakrāyudha mentioned in this inscription is evidently the same Cakrāyudha who received the sovereignty of Mahodaya from Dharmmapāla of Bengal, and this identity is made doubly certain by the phrase "*parāśrayakṛta-sphuṭa-nīca-bhāvaṁ.*" The inscription has since been edited by Pandit Hirānanda Sāstrī of the Archæological Survey, Northern Circle, and the verses about the conquests of Nagabhaṭa II run thus:—

Trayy = āspadasya sukṛtasya samṛddhim = icchur = yaḥ kṣatradhārā-vidhi-vaddha vali-prabandhaḥ,

Jitvā parāśraya-kṛta-sphuṭa-nīca-bhāvaṁ Cakrāyudhaṁ vinayanamra-pūrvvarājat. —verse 9.[2]

As a confirmation of the above statement came the verses of an unpublished grant of Amoghavarṣa I, now in the possession of Prof. Śrīdhara R. Bhandarkar, according to which during the victorious march of Govinda III, Dharmma and Cakrāyudha submitted of their own accord to that king:—

Himavat = parvvata-nirjjhar = āmbu turagaiḥ pītañ = ca gāḍhaṅ-gajair-ddhanitaṁ majjan-turyakair = dviguṇitaṁ bhuyopi tat-kandare, svayam = ev = opanatau ca yasya mahatas = tau Dharmma-Cakrāyudhau Himavān-kīrttisarūpatām-upagatas-tat = kīrttinārāyaṇaḥ.—verse 23.[3]

As Nāgabhaṭa is mentioned in the preceding verse there remains no doubt about the identity of Dharmma and Cakrāyudha and the Cakrāyudha and the King of Bengal of the Gwalior inscription. He is the very same person who was seated on the throne of Mahodaya or Kanauj by Dharmmapāla of Bengal and who was defeated by the Gurjara king Nāgabhaṭa at the same time as the Pāla king. The mention of Nāgabhaṭa in the preceding verse makes this identification doubly certain:—

Sa Nāgabhaṭa-Candragupta-nṛpayor-yaśo(?) r-yaṁ raṇe svahāryam = apahārya dhairya-vikalān-ath-onmulayan.

Yasor-jjanaparo nṛpān-svàbhuvi śāli sasyān-iva puṇaḥ punaratiṣthipat-svapada eva c = ānyān = api.—verse 22,[4]

So it is evident that the Kings Nāgabhaṭa II and Govinda III were the contemporaries of Dharmmapāla and Cakrāyudha. We possess a certain date for Nāgabhaṭa II, in the Buchkala inscription; the Vikrama year 872=815 A.D.[5]

---

1 Nachrichten von der Konigl. Ges. der Wiss. zu Gottingen, Phil. Hist. klasse, 1905, p. 301.

2 Ann. Rep. Archl. Surv., 1903—04, pp. 281 and 284.

3 J.B.B.R.A.S., Vol. XXII, pt. LXI, p 118.

4 Ibid.

5 Epi. Ind., Vol. IX, p. 198.

Govinda III's certain dates range from 794 to 813 A. D.[1] Consequently Dharmmapāla must be placed in the last decades of the eighth and the first decades of the ninth century A. D.

The events of Dharmmapala's reign.

The most important event in the reign of Dharmmapāla is his conquest of Northern India. The Rāṣṭrakūṭa king Dhruva had driven the Gurjara invaders back into the desert and the Rāṣṭrakūṭa occupation of the country most probably did not last long, otherwise there would not have been any necessity of a fresh invasion under Govinda III. The whole of Northern India most probably relapsed into that restless state which necessitated the election of a strong ruler in Bengal On his accession, an able man like Dharmmapāla practically found the whole country at his mercy. The ancient race of Bhaṇḍi had been ousted from the throne by Vatsarāja, Nāgabhaṭa's father, and a king named Indrāyudha was reigning at Mahodaya or Kanauj in the Vikrama year 705=783 A. D. It may be that he also belonged to the family of Bhaṇḍi. When we remember that according to the verse of the Bhagalpur grant of Nārāyaṇapāla, Dhrammapāla ousted a king of Kanauj named Indrarāja and gave the kingdom to Cakrāyudha, we feel certain that this Indrāyudha is no other than the Indrarāja of the Bhagalpur grant.

Dharmmapāla's Northern Indian campaign must have begun some time after 783 A. D. In the Jaina Harivaṁśa Purāṇa we find that in the year 705 of the Śaka era Indrāyudha was ruling in the North, Śrī-Vallabha in the South, the Lord of Avanti in the East, and Vatsarāja in the West:—

Śākeṣvabdaśateṣu saptasu diśāṁ pañchottareṣūttarāṁ
Pātīndrāyudhanāmni Kṛṣṇanṛpaje Śrīvallabhe dakṣiṇāṁ,
Pūrvaṁ Śrīmad-Avantī-bhubhṛti nṛpe Vatsādirāje parāṁ
Sorya nāmādhimaṇḍale jayayute vīre varāhe vati.

We know already from the Wani and Radhanpur grants that Dhruva, Śri Vallabha and Vatsarāja were contemporaries. In the year 783 Dhruva must have been in his old age, and long before that he must have driven Vatsarāja back into the desert country from Kanauj and Bengal as the latter is only mentioned as ruler of the West. Again, as Indrarāja or Indrāyudha was reigning in the North in 783 A. D., so Dharmmapāla's Northern Indian campaign must have taken place after that year. As has been already stated above, Dhruva and Vatsarāja seem to have had very long reigns. The invasion of Northern India by these two kings seems to have taken place during the earlier parts of their reigns. Bengal most probably enjoyed about fifty years' respite from foreign invasions before Dharmmapāla came to the throne. Though Indrāyudha, the contemporary of Dhruva and Vatsarāja, was dispossessed of his throne by Dharmmapāla, yet it appears that both of these kings died before Dharmmapāla's accession, as their sons, Nāgabhaṭa II and Govinda III, are mentioned in the inscriptions as his contemporaries. The first act of Dharmmapāla

[1] Ibid., Vol. VII, App. II, p. 3.

after his accession seems to have been the invasion of Kanauj. The exact cause of this invasion has not been revealed to us by any of the records discovered up to date. Most probably the existence of the weak kingdom on his western frontier tempted him to lead an invasion into the heart of the middle country. The result of this invasion is already well known. Indrāyudha, the old king,—old he must have been as he was to some extent the contemporary of the Rāṣṭrakūṭa Dhruva and the Gurjara Vatsarāja,—was deposed. Dharmmapāla set up a nominee of his own, named Cakrāyudha, who was most probably the king of the Pañcāla Country. The last supposition is based on the fact that in the Khalimpur grant it is stated that the Elders of the Pañcāla Country rejoiced at his election. This selection finally proved to be a very costly one for Dharmmapāla. In the famous historical verse of the Khalimpur grant we find that the Kuru, Yadu, Yavana, Avantī, Gandhāra, Kīra, Bhoja, Matsya and Madra kings had to agree to the selection of Cakrāyudha as the king of Kanauj or Mahodaya. This means, in plain language, that Dharmmapāla had to defeat these kings, and then to force his nominee on them. Consequently we must acknowledge that Dharmmapāla conquered or overran Eastern Punjab and Sindh (*Kuru* and *Yadu*), Western Punjab and the North-Western Frontier Provinces (*Yavana* and *Gandhāra*), Kangra (*Kīra*), Malwa (*Avantī*), and North-Eastern Rajputana (*Bhoja* and *Matsya*). The Madras are mentioned in the Mahābhārata as living outside the pale of Aryan civilization, and most probably the country meant is some part of Afghanistan.[1]

Conquest of Kanauj and displacement of Indrāyudhā.

The accession of Cakrāyudha on the throne of Kanauj was not satisfactory to Nāgabhaṭa II, the king of the Gurjaras. We know from the 9th verse of the Gwalior inscription of Bhoja I, that Nāgabhaṭa II defeated Cakrāyudha. According to the 10th verse of the same inscription he is said to have defeated the King of Bengal also:—

> *Dūrvvāra-vairı-vara-vāraṇa-vāji-vārayān = augha-saṁghaṭana-ghora-ghan—āndha-kāraṁ,*
> *Nirjjitya Vaṁgapatim = āvirabhūd = vivasvān = udyan = n-iva tri-jagad-eka-vikāśa-kośaḥ.*—verse 10.[2]

It is evident that Dhammapāla tried his best to support his protegee. In so doing he must have suffered a serious reverse at the hands of the Gurjara king. In this condition both Dharmmapāla and Cakrāyudha sought the help of the Rāṣṭrakūṭa Emperor Govinda III. This is proved by the 23rd verse of the unpublished grant of Amoghavarṣa I in the possession of Mr. S. R. Bhandarkar. Being solicited by the most influential king of Northern India and his subordinate, the king of one of the oldest cities in India, the Rāṣṭrakūṭa monarch led a campaign against the powerful Gurjaras. The result of this campaign has already been stated above while quoting the 23rd verse of the unpublished grant of Amoghavarṣa I.

1 Ind. Ant., Vol. XXXV, p. 17.

2 Arch. Survey Rep., 1903-04, p. 281.

The defeat inflicted upon the Gurjaras by the Rāṣṭrakūṭa Emperor had a very lasting effect. Govinda III made his nephew, the Mahāsāmantādhipati Karkarāja II of the Gujarat Branch of the Rāṣṭrakūṭa family, a door-bar for the country of the Gurjaras, which we learn from the verse of the Baroda grant of Karkarāja quoted above. Besides the unpublished grant of Amoghavarṣa I, we have further evidence of the defeat of a Gurjara king by Govinda III. In the Radhanpur grant of Govinda III it is stated that the Gurjara king fled on hearing of the approach of Govinda III, as the rainy season flies away on the approach of autumn;—

> *Saṁdhāy=āśu śilīmukhāṁ sva-samayāṁ va(ba)nāsanasy=opari prāp:aṁ varddhita-vaṁ(baṁ)dhujīva-vibhavaṁ padm-ābhivṛddhy-anvitaṁ.*
>
> *Sannakṣatram=udīkṣya yaṁ śarad-ṛtuṁ parjanyavad=Gurjaro naṣṭah kv= āpi bhayāt=tathā na samaraṁ svapne=pi paśyed=yathā.*—verse 15.[1]

The dream of having a capital at Kanauj, which had impelled more than one Gurjara King to invade Northern India, was over. The Mahāsāmanta became such an efficient door-bar that the Gurjaras were confined to the desert tracts of Rajputana for more than two generations. Dharmmapāla and Cakrāyudha were left in undisputed possession of their territories. Further mention of this triangular struggle between the Pālas, Gurjaras and the Rāṣṭrakūṭas is to be found in two inscriptions of Mahendrapāla, edited by the late Dr. Kielhorn just before his death. In these grants it is stated that Vāhukadhavala, a feudatory of the Gurjara Emperor Mahendrapāla, but a Cālukya by descent, defeated a king named Dharmma. Now as Vāhukadhavala was the third in ascent from Balavarman, the contemporary of Mahendrapāla, it is probable that he was a contemporary of Nāgabhaṭa II, who, as we have seen above, was the contemporary of Dharmmapāla of Bengal. So it now appears to be certain that the king Dharmma defeated by Vāhukadhavala was no other than Dharmmapāla of Bengal, who was fighting for his lost prestige in Northern India. In his article on the Una grant of Mahendrapāla, Dr. Kielhorn says that as Balavarman was a contemporary of Mahendrapāla and lived in 893 A.D., so his grandfather Vāhukadhavala must be the contemporary of Bhoja I.[2] But this is hardly possible as king Dharmmapāla must have preceded Bhoja I to some extent at any rate. As Balavarman, as well as his son, Avanivarman II, were the contemporaries of Mahendrapāla so it becomes certain that Balavarman was advanced in age when Mahendrapāla came to the throne. So Balavarman himself must be taken to be the contemporary of the Emperor Bhoja I. Consequently Avanivarman I becomes the contemporary of Rāmabhadra and Vāhukadhavala of Nāgabhaṭa II. This statement is amply supported by the fact that Nāgabhaṭa II had a long war with Dharmmapāla of Bengal. Vāhukadhavala is also said in Mahendrapāla's grants to have defeated the Karṇṇāṭa Army. As Dr. Kielhorn has suggested, the Karṇṇāṭas mentioned are really Rāṣṭrakūṭas. Most probably Vāhukadhavala defeated some portion of the Rāṣṭrakūṭa forces during the Northern Indian campaign of Govinda III.

We know from the Nilgund inscription of Amoghavarṣa I, that some time during

---

1 Epi. Ind. Vol. VI, p. 244.

2 Epi. Ind., Vol. IX, p. 3.

the campaign of Dharmmapāla and Govinda III against Nāgabhaṭa II, the Pāla and Rāṣṭrakūṭa kings fell out and in the struggle which ensued Dharmmapāla was defeated. This must have taken place after the defeat of Nāgabhaṭa II by the confederate armies:—

Kerala-Mālava-Gauḍān = sa-Gurjjarā[ṁ]ś = Citrakūṭagiridu[r]-ggasthān baddhvā Kāñcīśān = atha sa Kīrttinārāyaṇo jātaḥ.[1]

Dharmmapāla must have reigned for at least thirty-two years as his Khalimpur grant is dated in that year. Tārānātha says that he ruled for sixty-four years, which is impossible as we shall see in the following pages. The late Dr. Kielhorn was also of opinion that Dharmmapāla had a long reign.[2] In the Monghyr grant it is stated that Dharmmapāla married the daughter of the Rāṣṭrakūṭa chief Parabala, a lady named Raṇṇādevi.[3] Recently Dr. Kielhorn has published an inscription found on a pillar at Pathari, in the Native State of Bhopal in Central India. According to this inscription a king of the Rāṣṭrakūṭas named Parabala was reigning in the Vikrama year 917=861 A.D.[4] This Parabala is most probably the father-in-law of Dharmmapāladeva. So if Parabala married his daughter to the Pāla king, the latter must have had reigned for a very long time. Parabala and his father were very long-lived men. His father Karkarāja defeated a king named Nāgāvaloka, who was a contemporary of Chāhamāna Guvāka I of Sākambharī and one of whose grants is dated in the year 813 of the Vikrama era=756 A.D.[5] Dharmmapāla had a son named Tribhuvanapāla, who is mentioned in the Kha'impur grant as the *dūtaka*, and who seems to have died during the lifetime of his father as Dharmmapāla was succeeded by his second son Devapāladeva after a reign of about forty years.

Length of reign, and relations.

No coins of Dharmmapāla have been discovered as yet, and the only other inscription of Dharmmapāla besides the Khalimpur grant is a small votive inscription of the 26th year of his reign, found at Bodh-Gaya in the Gaya district of Bengal. The sculpture, on which the inscription has been incised, was removed to the Indian Museum in 1895 when Mr. Broadley's collection of antiquities was sent to Calcutta by the order of the Government of Bengal. The inscription was published in 1908 by Pandit Nilmoni Chakravartti, Professor of Pali and Sanskrit in the Presidency College, Calcutta. It records the erection of a four-faced Mahādeva in a place called Campaśāyatana, by a man named Keśava, the son of a sculptor named Ujvala, and the excavation of a tank at the cost of three thousand drammas, in the 26th regnal year of Dharmmapāla.[6] His Khalimpur grant was issued from Pāṭaliputra. It is well known that he is the king of Bengal repeatedly referred to in the Rāṣṭrakūṭa and Gurjara records. In the Monghyr grant of his son Devapāla, Dharmmapāla's followers are said to have bathed at Kedāra, and at the mouth of the Ganges during his expeditions, and this bears out the statements made in the

---

1 Ibid., Vol. VI, p. 103.
2 Nach. Kon. Ges. der Wiss. zu Gottengen, 1905, p. 303.
3 Ind. Ant., Vol. XXI, p. 255.
4 Epi. Ind., Vol. IX, p. 250.
5 Ibid., p. 231, note 4.
6 J.A.S.B., Vol. IV, New Series, p. 102.

Khalimpur grant. This grant was issued in his 32nd year and records the grant of the villages named Krauñcaśvabhra, Māḍhāsāmmalī and Pālitaka in the Vyāghrataṭī *maṇḍala* of the Mahantāprakāśa *viṣaya*, and Gopippalī of the Āmraṣaṇḍikā *maṇḍala* of the Sthālikkaṭa *viṣaya*, all of which were situated in the Pauṇḍravardhana *bhukti*, to the temple of the god Nunna-Nārāyaṇa at Śubhasthalī, at the request of his feudatory, the *Mahāsāmantādhipati* Nārāyaṇavarmman, which was communicated to the king by the Prince Tribhuvanapāla.

CHAPTER III.

THE STRUGGLE WITH THE PRATĪHĀRAS.

For a long time after the Northern Indian campaign of Govinda III, the Rāṣṭrakūṭa, Bengal enjoyed immunity from Gurjara invasions. The Rāṣṭrakūṭas had barred the Gurjaras so effectively in their desert country, that for the next two or three generations, the Gurjara kings were obliged to remain content with their former boundaries. It was not till the reign of the Gurjara Emperor Bhoja I, Mihira or Ādivarāha, that we hear of a Gurjara invasion of Bengal. After his succession to the throne, Devapāla was engaged in several lengthy campaigns, and pushed his conquests as far as the Himalayas in the North and the Vindhya Hills in the South :—

Bhrāmyadbhir = vijaya-krameṇa karibhiḥ svām = eva Vindhy-āṭavīm = uddāma-plavamāna-vāṣpa-payaso dṛṣṭāḥ punar = bāndhavāḥ. Kambojeṣu cā yasya vāji-yuvabhir = dhvast-ānyarāj-aujaso heṣā-miśrita hari-heṣita-ravāḥ kāntāś-ciram vikṣitaḥ.—ll.—19-20.[1]

He met with considerable success in his wars, and we find a corroboration of this statement in an inscription incised at the request of the grandson of his minister, Darbhapāṇi Miśra. The Badal pillar inscription records that " By his (Darbhapāṇi's) policy the illustrious prince Devapāla made tributary the earth as far as Revā's parent, whose pile of rocks are moist with the rutting juice of elephants, as far as Gauri's father, the mountain which is whitened by the rays of Īśvara's moon, and as far as the two oceans, whose waters are red with the rising and the setting of the sun ":—

Ā Revā-janakān = mataṅgaja-madastimyac-chila-saṅghater = ā-gaurī-pitur = īśvar endu-kiranaiḥ puṣyat = sitimno gireḥ,
Marttaṇḍās-tamay-oday-āruṇa-jalād-ā-vārirāśi-dvayān = nītyā yasya bhuvaṁ cakāra karadāṁ Śrī-Devapālo nṛpaḥ.—verse 5.[2]

In the very same inscription another verse refers to the campaigns of the same king and mentions the names of his antagonists in detail. This verse has been assigned to Vigrahapāla I by Mahāmahopādhyāya Hara Prasāda Śāstrī,[3] but in my humble opinion it refers to the king Devapāla, for the simple reason that the verse referring to Śūrapāla, the next king after Devapāla, according to the Badal pillar inscription, is placed after it. According to this inscription both Darbhapāṇi and his grandson Kedāramiśra were the contemporaries of Devapāla. Someśvara, the son of Darbhapāṇi and the father of Kedāramiśra, was

---

[1] Ind. Ant., Vol. XXI, p. 255. [2] Epi. Ind., Vol. II, p. 162. [3] Mem. A.S.B, Vol. III, p. 8.

most probably a general.[1] Kedāramiśra continued as minister under Śūrapāla I or Vigrahapāla I, and his son Guravamiśra was the minister of Nārāyaṇpāla. The second verse in the Badal pillar inscription about the campaigns of Devapāla runs as follows:—

Utkīlit-otkala-kulaṁ hṛta-hūṇa-garvvaṁ kharvvīkṛta-draviḍa-gurjjaranātha-darppaṁ,
Bhū-pīṭham=abdhi-raśan=ābharaṇamvubhoja Gauḍeśvaraś=ciram=upāsya dhiyaṁ yadīyāṁ—verse 13.

"Attending to his (Kedāramiśra's) wise counsel the lord of Gauḍa long ruled the sea-girt earth, having eradicated the race of the Utkalas, humbled the pride of the Hūṇas, and scattered the conceit of the rulers of Draviḍa and Gurjjara."

Devapāla, his wars.

The invasion of Utkala is a new point, but the fight with the Hūṇas perhaps is the same as that with the Kambojas referred to in the Monghyr grant. We know from an independent source that there was a war with the Drāviḍas, i.e. the Rāṣṭrakūṭas. In the Nilgund inscription Amoghavarṣa I, it is stated that he was "worshipped by the lords of Vaṅga, Aṅga, Magadha, Mālava and Veṅgi":—

Ari-nṛpati-makuṭa-ghaṭṭita-caranas=sakala-bhuvana-vandita-śauryyaḥ,
Vaṁg-āṁga-Magadha-Mālava-Veṁgīśair=arccito=tiśayadhavalaḥ. 7-8.[2]

Amoghavarṣa I seems to have been the contemporary of Devapāla as we know that his father Govinda III was of Dharmmapāla. The first three names: Vaṅga, Aṅga and Magadha, must refer to one and the same kingdom as we know from inscriptions that Vaṅga, Aṅga and Magadha were under Devapāla, viz. the Monghyr grant and the Ghosrawan inscription. The Rāṣṭrakūṭa invasion was most probably over within a very short time, like those under the predecessors of Amoghavarṣa I, and at its close, in spite of the reverses, Devapāla was left master of Northern India. The war with the Gurjaras was either followed by the invasion of Amoghavarṣa I, or itself followed that. In either case it is quite clear that the Gurjara king Rāmabhadra suffered this reverse at the hands of this king of Bengal, for neither in the Gurjara copper-plate grants nor in their stone inscriptions are any victories assigned to him.

During the reign of Devapāla, a Brāhmaṇa named Vīradeva, an inhabitant of Nagarahāra, came on a pilgrimage to the Mahābodhi and paid a visit to the Yaśovarmmapura Vihāra. During his stay in Magadha, Devapāla heard of him and he was made the principal abbot of Nālandā.[3] The Monghyr grant was issued to record the grant of a village named Meṣika, in the Krimilā *Viṣaya*, and the Śrī-nagara *bhūkti*, to a brāhmaṇa named Vihekarāta, of the Aupamanyava gotra and the Āśvalāyana *Śākhā*, in the 33rd year of the king. The *dūtaka* of the grant was the king's son Rājyapāla. There is a vast mass of MSS. literature

---

1 Epi. Ind., Vol II, p. 162, verse 9. 2 Ibid., Vol. VI, p. 103. 3 Ind. Ant., Vol. XVII, p. 309.

in Bengal recording the descent of Brāhmaṇas. For the most part these MSS. are carelessly copied and hardly reliable, save for the names and descent of Brāhmaṇas. These records are said to contain historical allusions. Devapāla is mentioned in one of these genealogical works, the old Kārikā of Hari-Miśra-Ghaṭaka.[1] But it is quite possible that the name is a modern interpolation, added to prove the authenticity of the work. The śloka itself as quoted by Babu Nagendra Nātha Vasu runs as follows :—

Inscriptions and Mss. records.

Kṣmāpāla-pratibhūr-bhuvaḥ patir-abhūd Gauḍe ca rāṣṭre tataḥ,
Rājā-bhūt pravalaḥ sadaiva śaraṇaḥ Śrī-Devapālas=tataḥ.

The Prince Rājyapāla was made a Yuvarāja before the grant of the copper-plate in the 33rd regnal year, but he must have died during the lifetime of his father as we find that the king Devapāla was succeeded by Vigrahapāla I, the son of his cousin Jayapāla and the grandson of Vakpāla, the younger brother of Dharmmapāla. In the Badal pillar inscription, the next king after Devapāla is named Śūrapāla. But these two names belong to one and the same person as we shall have to see later on. In the Monghyr grant the date is given as the 33rd regnal year, but according to Tārānātha, Devapāla is said to have reigned forty-eight years. This is most probably incorrect, though we find that both Darbhapāṇi and his grandson Kedāramiśra were his ministers and contemporaries. Devapāla's successor was Vigrahapāla I or Śūrapāla I, whose father Jayapāla had led the expedition against the king of Utkala or Orissa at the request of his cousin and conquered Prāgjyotiṣa for him.[2] Vigrahapāla I is no doubt the same as the Śūrapāla mentioned in the Badal pillar inscription because it is the only name mentioned between Devapāla and Nārāyaṇapāla, and again in the Bhagalpur grant, Vigrahapāla's name is the only one mentioned between Devapāla and Nārāyaṇapāla. Moreover in the Manahali grant of Madanapāla we do not find the name of Śūrapāla before or close to the name of Nārāyaṇapāla. Had there been a different prince of the name of Śūrapāla, his name would surely have been mentioned in it as that inscription contains almost all the names of the Pāla dynasty. Only two small inscriptions of Śūrapāla I have been discovered as yet. Both of them are dated in the second year of this king and record the erection of images at the Vihāra in Uddaṇḍapura by an old Buddhist monk named Pūrṇadāsa. These two inscriptions have been assigned to Śūrapāla II on palæographical grounds by Prof. Nilmoni Chakravartti but that is hardly tenable, as inscriptions of Mahīpāla I and Rāmapāla are written in Proto-Bengali character and it is hardly possible that the inscriptions of Rāmapāla's brother should be written in the acute-angled form of Nagari characters. The name of the Vihāra was read by Prof. Chakravartti as Uddaṇḍacuṛa,[3] but in reality it is Uddaṇḍapura.[4] Uddaṇḍapura is the ancient name of the modern town of Bihar. It

His successor and relations. Length of reign.

Vigrahapāla I or Surapāla I.

[1] J.A.S.B., Pt. I, 1896, p. 21.
[2] Ind. Ant., Vol. XV, p. 305, v. 6.
[3] J.A.S.B., N.S., Vol. IV, p. 108.
[4] Mem. A.S.B., Vol III, p. 13.

is mentioned as Adwand Bihar in the Ṭabaqāt-i-Nāṣiri of Minhāj-ud-dīn[1] and as Uddaṇḍapura in another mediæval inscription in the town of the Gaya in Bengal.[2] The Tibetan historian Lama Tārānatha mentions it as Otantapura,[3] which is the nearest approach to the Sanskrit Uddaṇḍapura. Śūrapāla I or Vigrahapāla I married Lajjādevi, the daughter of the Haihaya king of Tripuri.[4] Vigrahapāla's father, Jayapāla, was a Hindu by inclination, as after his father Vak-pāla's death he is said to have performed the funeral ceremony according to Hindu rites. Umāpati, a learned Brahmana of Kāñjivilvī, is said to have got the Mahādāna on that occasion. The fact is recorded in a commentary on the *Chandogapariśiṣṭa* named *Pariśiṣṭa-prakāśa* by Umāpati's grandson, Nārāyaṇa :—

Kṣmāpālāj = Jayapālataḥ sa hi Mahāśrāddham prabhutam.
Mahādānam c-arthi-gaṇ = ārhaṇ = ārdra-hṛdayaḥ praty-agrahīt puṇyavān.—verse 8.[5]

The name of the village where Umāpati lived is given as Kāñjivindā in the 2nd verse, but it is clearly a mistake for Kanjivilva, the name of a well-known town. Nothing is known about the other relatives of this king, besides his son Nārāyaṇapāla who succeeded him. The votive inscriptions mentioned above were incised in the 2nd year of the king and most probably Vigrahapāla I or Śūrapāla I had a very short reign.

Nārāyaṇapāla succeeded to the throne in very troublesome times. The Gurjaras, after their long confinement in the desert, were issuing again for the conquest of Northern India, and this time they were destined to succeed and to make Mahodaya or Kānyakubja their capital. Bhoja I succeeded his father Rāmabhadra and at the beginning his kingdom seems to have consisted of the ancestral lands of the Gurjara-Pratīhāras. Step by step Bhoja advanced towards the North. Kanauj or Mahodaya became his capital as several of his grants were issued from that place. It is not known from whom the Gurjara king wrested Kanauj, and it may be that it was taken either from the Pālas or one of their contemporaries. Nothing is known about the state of Uttarāpatha or Northern India about this time, but it is certain that the Pālas lost much of their territorial possessions during this period. Bhoja I invaded Bengal and defeated the king disastrously. The war with Bengal is mentioned in his Gwalior inscription:—

Bhoja I and his war with the Palas.

Yasya vairi bṛhad = baṅgān = dahataḥ kopa-vahṇinā.
Pratāpād = arṇṇasāṁ rāśīn = pātur = vvaitṛṣṇam = āvabhau.—verse 21.[6]

This invasion must have taken place late in the reign of Bhoja I, as it must have taken him some time to be seated on the throne, advance towards Kanauj, conquer it and then invade Magadha and Vaṅga. The invasion is recorded in another Pratihāra inscription found at Māndor in Jodhpur. Kakkuka, whose brother Bauka's

1 Tabaqat-i-Nasiri (Bib. Ind.), p. 491.
2 Cunningham, Arch. Surv. Rep., Vol. III, p. 128.
3 Ibid.
4 Ind. Ant., Vol. XV, p. 305, v. 9.
5 Eggeling-Cat., Skt. MSS. in Ind. Office Lib., Pt. I, pp. 92-3.
6 Ann. Rep. Arch. Surv. Ind., 1903-04, pp. 282-84.

inscription is dated Vikrama Saṁvat 918=861 A.D., states that his father Kakka gained fame in a fight with the Gauḍas at Mudgagiri :—

Tatopi Śrīyutaḥ Kakkaḥ puttro jāto mahāmatiḥ.
Yaśo Mudgagirau labdhaṁ, yena Gauḍaiḥ samaṁ raṇe.—*verse* 24.[1]

Kakka seems to have accompanied Bhoja in his expedition against Bengal. As his son Bauka was alive in 861 A.D.,[2] Bhoja I and Kakka must have invaded Bengal a few years earlier, and this invasion must have taken place during the earlier years of Nārāyaṇapāla.

The statements of the Gwalior inscription of Bhoja I and the Mandor inscription of the Pratīhāra Kakkuka lead one to believe that there was a great war between the first Pratīhāra Emperor Bhoja I and the Pāla Emperor Vigrahapāla I or Nārāyaṇapāla of Gauḍa and Vaṅga. This fact coupled with the discovery at least of three inscriptions mentioning the reign of the Emperor Mahendrapāla, the son of Bhoja I, in Magadha of Southern Bihar and one copper-plate in Tirhut, proves that the Province of Magadha was for a time added to the vast Empire of the Pratīhāras, either during the war of Bhoja I or after it.

We have positive evidence of the fact that the city of Gayā was in the possession of Nārāyaṇapāla up to the seventh year of his reign, because in that year a man named Bhāṇḍadeva erected a monastery for ascetics in that city. Up to the seventeenth year of Nārāyaṇapāla, Mudgagiri was in his possession as his grant was issued from that place in that year. From this grant we learn that at least a part of Tīrabhūkti or Mithilā continued to be in the possession of Nārāyaṇapāla.[3] The Pratīhāra Kakka most probably gained renown during the siege of the famous fort of Mudgagiri or Mungir.

Invasion of Amoghavarṣa I.

It appears that during the long reigns of Amoghavarṣa I and Bhoja I,—and they were to some extent contemporaries,—the Gurjaras had not come into collision with the Rāṣṭrakūṭas. In the Sirur and Nilgund inscriptions of Amoghavarṣa I, that monarch claims to have been worshipped by the kings of Vaṅga, Aṅga, Magadha, Mālava and Veṅgi :—

Ari-nṛpati-makuṭa-ghaṭṭita-caraṇas=sakala bhuvana bandita śauryyaḥ.
Vaṅg-Āṅga-Magadha-Mālava-Veṁgīśair=arccito=tiśayadhavalaḥ.[4]
-*verse* 6 *Nilgund inscription and verse* 5 *Sirur inscription.*[5]

The kings of Vaṅga, Aṅga and Magadha were most probably one and the same person, one of the Pālas, either Vigrahapāla I or Nārāyaṇapāla. Amoghavarṣa I must have invaded Magadha and Vaṅga through Orissa, or otherwise he must have come into conflict with the Gurjaras who were then occupying most of Northern India, but of this no record has been discovered up to date.

But as we have seen above, the Gurjaras succeeded in annexing Magadha and most probably Tīrabhūkti or Tirhut permanently to their dominions and succeeded in keeping them till the rise of the Cedis under Karṇṇadeva, when Mahīpāla I

---

1 J.R.A.S., 1894, pp. 3 & 7. 2 Ibid., 1895, p. 515. 3 Ind. Ant., Vol. XV, p. 306, l. 30.
4 Epi. Ind., Vol. VI, p. 103. 5 Ibid., Vol. VII, p. 205.

annexed Magdha to his territories. The Rāṣṭrakūṭa invasion was not a lasting one, like the previous ones, and, at the close of the war, the Gurjjara-Pratīhāras re-occupied Magadha.

According to the Bhagalpur grant, up to the seventeenth year of the king Mudgagiri was in his occupation. After that nothing is known about him. He was succeeded by his son Rājyapāladeva. The names of the other relations of the king are not known. The earliest record of Nārāyaṇapāla is the Gayā inscription of the seventh year. This is at present in the courtyard of the Viṣṇupāda temple in Gaya City. Its discovery was announced by the late Sir Alexander Cunningham in his reports, with a drawing.[1] As this inscription has never before been properly edited, I edit it from the original:—

Inscriptions of Narayanapala.

1. *Oṁ namo Puruṣottamāya namaḥ* || *Oṁ jayati jagati nāthaḥ prasphurac=cārumūrttir =jagad-ari-vinihantā Śrī-mad=eko murāris=tadanu-muni-janoya*[*ṁ*] *sthira-saṁkleśa-rāśiḥ sphura-*
2. *-d=amala-guṇāyāṁ dhyāna-vṛttau sthirātmā* || *Prodbhūt-āti-darppa-pravala-mana-saṁtrāsa-hetu-svabhāvaṁ Kṛtv-aitan-nārasiṅghaṁ sphuṭa-vikaṭa-saṭam rūpam =aty-ugra-raudraṁ* । *ye-*
3. *-n=odīrṇṇaḥ pṛthivyām khara-nakhara-karair=bhedito daityarājaḥ Śrī-mān= lokaikanātho bhuvana-hita-vidhātā pātu yuṣmān=sa viṣṇuḥ* || *Śrī-mān=aśeṣa-śubha-saṁbhṛta-cāru-mū-*
4. *-rttiḥ bhadraḥ sunirmmala-dhiyāṁ pravaro Śrīgrāha* (?) । *Prāptodayādita kule sukṛti vabhūva yo Vāmadeva iti sarvva-jagat=pratītaḥ* । *Tasy=ātmajaḥ priya-tamo viduṣāṁ samā-*
5. *-sīt yaṁ Sīhadevam-iti vandhu-jano juhāva* [।] *Tasyābhavat=sutavaro varadharm-mavṛttiḥ sammānito gurujanair=api Vappadevaḥ* || *Sarvvārtha-siddhikaraṇ-aika -nidhāna-bhūtā sau-*
6. *-ndarya-garbha-rucir-āmala-rūpa-saṁpat patnī ca tasya kamal=eva sadā praśastā khyātā bhavaj=jagati Vallabhadevy=at=īṣṭā* || *Tābhyām=ajanyām=ajāyata suto-mala-*
7. *-dharmma-vṛttir=vvāk-kāya-citta-kṛta-saṁyamano-bhimānī*[।]*Brahm-opavīta-carite vrata-saṅgata-śrīḥ yo Bhāṇḍadeva iti pūrvvam=iha pratītaḥ* || *Vidyul=lolām kṣaṇa-pariṇatīṁ*
8. *saṁskṛtānāṁ viditvā janmottrāsād=amala-bhuvana prāptum=abhyudgatena* [।] *yen=āty=arthaṁ sukṛta-matibhis=sevite dhyāna-mārgge ceto-nyastaṁ* [*su*]*vima-lamalaṁ jñānam=āsvādanā-*
9. *-ya* || *Ten=āneka-dvija-jana bhuvi prema-vṛttyā Gayāyāṁ Śrī-mād=eṣo yatiṣu vihita* [*ḥ*] *sad-guṇ-āvāsa-vāsaḥ jñātaṁ śreyo yad=amala-guṇaṁ vrahma-caryāśra-meṇa tenā-*
10. *stvataj=jagad=amalinaṁ kṣīṇa-saṁkleśa-rāśiḥ* || *Cātur-vvidyam-samastaṁ prasa-mita-kaluṣaṁ vrahma-saṁnyasta-vṛttiṁ Śrīmantaṁ sat=kriyātmā prathita-pṛthu-guṇaṁ prārthaya-*

---

[1] Cunningham, Arch. Surv. Rep., Vol. III, p. 120, No. 6, pt. XXXVI.

11. *-ty-eṣa maunī Bhuyāl=lokos mita-śrīḥ para-kṛta-sukṛtaiḥ pālane rakṣaṇe ca tat=karttavyaṁ bhavadbhiḥ sthiravamala-guṇaḥ syānnivāya-yathāyaṁ* ‖ *Sad=vṛtt-=āmala-vṛ-*

12. *-ttibhiḥ sphuṭataraṁ jātādaraiḥ sarvvataḥ sarvvān=etā[n] bhāvina[ḥ] pārthivendrā bhūyo bhūyo jācaty=eṣa maunī sāmāny=oyaṁ dharmma-śetur=nārāṇ [āṁ] kāle kāle pā-*

13. *-laneyo bhavadbhiḥ* [‖] *Vyāṅgānārya-vahis=tapodhana-janaiḥ sthātavyam=atr=āśrame* । *Ity=etat=vratadhāribhir=niyamitaṁ bhuyād=yathā-nānyathā* । *Karttavyaṁ tad=ih=āmalaṁ pri-*

14. *-yatamair=viprair=Gayāvāsibhiḥ* ‖ *Sphuratu kīrttir=iyaṁ guṇa-śālinī sakala-satva-hit-odaya-hetave tapati yāvad=ayaṁ bhuvi bhāskaro himaka-*

15. *-reṇa sah=āmala-dīdhitiḥ* । *Śrī-Nārāyaṇapāladeva iti prāpt-odayo bhūpatiḥ bhūto bhūmi bhūjā [ṁ] śirobhir-amala yasy-ocita [ṁ] śāsanaṁ rājñas=ta-*

16. *-sya guṇ-ānalasya mahataḥ samvatsare saptame Vaiśākhyāṁ śubha-sambhṛtena vidhinā labdha pratiṣṭhīta-maṭha.*

The language of the inscription is very incorrect Sanskrit, like that of the Buddhist Sanskrit manuscripts of Nepal, and the record itself has been very carelessly incised. The purpose of the inscription is to record the erection of a monastery for Brāhmaṇical ascetics by a man named Bhāṇḍadeva in the seventh year of the king Nārāyaṇapāladeva, in the month of Vaiśākha. It opens with an invocation to Viṣṇu, in his Man-lion (Narasiṁha) incarnation and curiously enough it is at present outside the small temple of Narasiṁha, in the courtyard of the Viṣṇupāda temple, which, as we shall see later on, was certainly built during the reign of Nayapāladeva. It may mean however that the small temple of Narasiṁha was built by Bhāṇḍadeva near the monastery and was rebuilt during the time of Nayapāladeva. The genealogy of the builder is given as follows:—

VĀMADEVA,
married Vallabhadevī,
|
SIHADEVA,
|
VAPPADEVA,
|
BHĀṆḌADEVA.

Another small inscription of Nārāyaṇapāla was found by Pandit Vinoda Vihari Vidyavinoda of the Indian Museum, Calcutta, in the Inscription gallery of that Museum. He has published it in the journal of the Vaṅgiya Sāhitya Parishad.[1] It is incised on a long piece of carved stone, probably the portion of a pedestal. Most probably it came with the other sculptures from the Bihar Museum founded by Mr. Broadley, when that collection was shifted to Calcutta, according to the direc-

[1] Vangiya Sahitya-parishad-Patrika, Vol. XV, p. 13.

tions of the Government of Bengal. There is no record about it in the Office of the Indian Museum. I edit it from an excellent inked impression made for me by Babu Hari Das Datta, of the Archæological Survey, Eastern Circle, at the order of the late Dr. T. Bloch.

(1) *Om Samvat* 9 *Vaiśākha Śudi* 5 *Parameśvara-Śrī-Nārāyaṇapāladeva-rājye Andhra-vaiṣayika Śākya-bhikṣu-sthavira-Dharmmamitrasya*

(2) *yad=atra puṇyaṁ tad=bhavatv-ācāry=opādhyāya-mātā-pitṛ-pūrvvaṅgamaṁ kṛtvā sakala-satva-rāśer=anuttara-jñāna-prāptaya iti* ||

It records the erection of an image in the ninth year of the king Nārāyaṇapāla, in the month of Vaiśākha, by a Buddhist Elder, named Dharmmamitra, an inhabitant of the Andhra country.

The Bhagalpur grant of Nārāyaṇapāladeva was issued when the king was staying at Mudgagiri and records the grant of the village of Makuṭikā to the temple of Siva at Kalaśapota, which was situated in the Kakṣa *viṣaya*, of Tīrabhūkti, thus proving that up to that time Tīrabhūkti or modern Tirhut was under the Pāla kings. The *Dūtaka* of this grant was the Bhaṭṭa Pūṇyakīrtti, otherwise named Guravamiśra, who erected the *Garuḍa-stambha* at Badal. The other inscription is not dated. It was incised to record the erection of a stone monolith surmounted by an image of Garuḍa by the Bhaṭṭa Guravamiśra, the minister of the king. According to this inscription Guravamiśra was the minister of Nārāyaṇapāla, his father Kedāramiśra that of Śūrapāla, and Devapāla, his grandfather Someśvara, a general, and his great-grandfather Darbhapāṇi, the minister of Devapāla, while his great-great-grandfather Garga was the minister of Dharmmapāla. The synchronism is shown below.

Pāla Emperors.		Ministers
I Gopāla I,		
II Dharmmapāla,	Vākpāla,	Gargga,
		Darbhapāṇi,
III Devapāla.	Jayapāla,	
		Someśvara,
	Śūrapāla I IV or Vigrahapāla I,	Kedāramiśra,
	V Nārāyaṇapāla.	Guravamiśra.

Nothing is known about Nārāyaṇapala's son Rājyapāla, who succeeded him, save that he married the Rāṣṭrakūṭa princess Bhāgyadevī, the daughter of Tuṅga, most probably the same as the Tuṅga Dharmmāvaloka, whose inscription at Mahabodhi was published by the late Dr. Rajendra Lala Mitra in his Buddha-Gaya.[1] The verse about the marriage of Rājyapala is to be found in the Bangarh grant of Mahipāla I, Amgachi grant of Vigrahapāla III and the Manahali grant of Madanapāla.

[1] Buddha-Gaya, p. 195, pl. XL.

We learn from the position of the Badal pillar that the *Varendrī* or Northern Bengal was included in the kingdom of Nārāyaṇapāla, and after the loss of Magadha and Tīrabhūkti his son must have succeeded to a very small principality which was situated either in Rāḍhā (Western Bengal) or in the Vaṅga (Eastern Bengal) as we know from later records that about this time a Mongolian tribe invaded Northern Bengal through modern Sikkim or Bhutan and occupied Gauḍa. Later on we shall see that Gauḍa was in the occupation of Mongolians in the Śaka year 888=966 A.D. So the invasion must have taken place some fifty or hundred years earlier. These Mongolians are named Kāmbojas in a Sanskrit inscription. In the Mungir grant of Devapāla and the Badal pillar inscription, Devapāla is said to have fought the Kāmbojas, but this may refer to the Western Kāmbojas. The Mongolian or Kāmboja invasion of Northern India must have taken place just after Nārāyaṇapāla as no Pāla records have been found in Northern Bengal till the accession of Mahīpāla I.

Magadha was annexed by the Gurjara-Pratihāras to their dominions, and after Nārāyaṇapāla we find the names of the Gurjara princes in the votive inscriptions of Magadha. For a long time scholars have been at a loss to assign a place to a king named Mahendrapāla, several of whose inscriptions have been found in the Gayā District. All along he has been considered to be one of the Pālas of Bengal. The late Dr. F. Kielhorn also thought that he was one of the Pālas, and mentions him in a footnote in his list of the Pāla kings of Bengal.[1] Mr. V. A. Smith, in his recent article on the Pālas of Bengal, goes so far as to assert that he was the successor of Govindapāla, whose inscriptions are dated Vikrama Saṃvat 1232 and 1235, i.e. 1175 and 1178 A.D.[2] Mahāmahopādhyāya Hara Prasād Śastrī thinks that Mahendrapāla may have belonged to the Pāla dynasty.[3] Two inscriptions of this king are definitely known to have been discovered in the Gayā District. One of these were found at Rām-gayā, on the other side of the river Phalgu, just opposite the temple of Gadādhar at Gayā, while the other was found at Guneriya, a village near the Grand Trunk Road. Major Kittoe spoke of a third inscription of this king, but of that we shall have to speak later on. The first of the inscriptions of this king, the one at Rāmgayā, was examined by the late Sir Alexander Cunningham, and the first line was deciphered by him. According to him, the record is incised on the pedestal of the figures of the ten incarnations of Viṣṇu. Following Cunningham's description, the image was at last found in the walls of a modern temple of Śiva at Rāmgayā, and after great difficulties, a clear impression was secured. It was evident even at the first sight that the record was considerably older than the inscriptions of Govindapāla, Rāmapāla or even Mahīpāla I. The figures of the ten avatāras are now completely hidden by whitewash, but the pedestal has been cleared of it, and it was found that the record had been incised on the right half of it. Acute-angled characters of the ninth century A.D. had been used in it, and on no account can it be placed later than the tenth century. As the record has only been partially edited before, I take the opportunity of placing it on record :—

1 Epi. Ind., Vol. VIII, App. p. 18, note 2.
2 Ind. Ant., Vol. XXXVIII, p. 246.
3 Mem. A.S.B., Vol. III, p. 16.

(1) *Oṁ Samvat* 8 । *Śrī-Mahīndrapāla* । *rājyābhiṣe-*
(2) *-ka* । *Saüḍi Riṣi putra Sahadevasya.*

"Om, the year 8 (from) the coronation of Mahīndrapāla. (The gift) of Sahadeva, the son of the Riṣi (*Ṛṣi*) Sauḍi (*Sauri*)."

Mahendrapāla, in the ninth or tenth centuries A.D., immediately suggests the name of the son of Bhoja I, the great Pratihāra Emperor Mahendrapāladeva. A comparison with the Asni inscription of Mahīpāla confirmed me in the opinion that no other person than the great Pratihāra monarch was being referred to. The forms of *P* and *J* are very much similar to those used in Asni inscription and the Ghosrawan inscription of Devapāla. Moreover, the form of the name is identical with that used in the Asni inscription, where we find the name as *Mahīndrapāla*, and not Mahendrapāla as in other inscriptions. Dr. Fleet read this name as Mahīṣapāla.[1] I saw a beautiful impression of this inscription in the Allahabad exibition of 1910-11, and there the name is clearly legible as Mahīndrapāla. Another inscription of Mahendrapāla is to be found at Gunariya, near the Grand Trunk Road, in the Gayā District, which was brought to notice by Major Kittoe. Kittoe's drawing of the inscribed portion of the sculpture is very clear and the record can be edited from it:—

(1) *Ye dharmmā hetu prabhavā hetun =teṣāṁ ta-*
(2) *-thāgato hy = avadat teṣāṁca yo nirodho evaṁ vā-*
(3) *-dī mahāśramaṇaḥ* । *Samvat* 9 *Vaiśākha.*
(4) *śudī* 5 *Śrī-Guṇa-*
(5) *-carita Śrī-Mahīndrapā-*
(6) *-ladevarājye devadha-*
(7) *-rmmeyaṁ* . . .

Kittoe found a third inscription of this king somewhere in Bihār, but as he did not state the exact locality, it is no use searching for it. Some day it will come up as a new discovery of some one who chances to stumble on it. According to Major Kittoe this inscription was dated in the 19th year of the king:—

"One mentions the fact of the party having apostatized, and again returned to the worship of the Śākya, in the 19th year of the reign of Śrī Mahendrapāladeva."[2] There are two votive inscriptions of Mahendrapāladeva in the British Museum. One of these records the erection, most probably, of an image by a Buddhist monk named Kusuma in the ninth year of Mahendrapāla.[3] The nature of the contents of the other inscription is not known, but it is dated in the second year of Mahendrapāladeva. It may be that the third inscription mentioned by Major Kittoe, has found its way, by some means or other, into the British Museum. As for the reading of the date, there need not be any difficulty about that, as Kittoe's readings are invariably faulty. So we have definite proof that in the eight and ninth years of the king Mahendrapāla, Magadha formed an integral part of the Gurjara-Pratīhāra Empire, which at that time extended from the Arabian Sea to the Bay of Bengal.[4]

---

1 Ind. Ant., Vol. XVI, p. 174.
2 J.A.S.B., Vol. XVII, 1848 pt. I, p. 238.
3 Nachr. v. d. Konigl. Ges. d. Wis. z. Gotting., phil.-hist. Kl. 1904, pp. 210-11
4 Epi. Ind., Vol IX, p. 4

No inscriptions of Rajyapāla have been discovered as yet, and so nothing definite can be stated about the length or the events of his reign. According to the inscriptions of the later Pālas, he was succeeded by his son Gopāla II.

The British Museum possesses a Manuscript of the Aṣṭasāhasrika Prajñāpāramitā written in the 15th year of Gopāla II at the monastery of Vikramaśilā. Its colophon runs thus :—

Parameśvara-paramabhaṭṭāraka-paramasaugata-Mahārājādhirāja-Śrī-mad-Gopāladevapravarddhamāna-kalyāṇa-vijaya-rajy-etyādi samvat 15 *āsmine dine* 4 *Śrī-mad Vikramaśīla-deva-vihāre likhiteyaṁ bhagavati.*[1]

We possess two inscriptions of Gopāla II, and from these we learn that Magadha was temporarily recovered by the Pālas during the reign of this monarch. The first of these inscriptions was discovered by the late Sir Alexander Cunningham, at Bargaon in the Patna District, the ancient Nālandā.[2] It records the fact that an image of the goddess Vagīsvarī, at Nālandā, was covered with gold leaf by some unnamed personage in the first year of Gopaladeva.[3] The second inscription was discovered amidst the ruins of the Mahābodhi temple at Bodh-Gayā and records the erection of image of Buddha by a person named Śakrasena during the reign of Gopāladeva, no year being mentioned. These inscriptions prove that some time during the reign of Gopāla II, South Bihār or Magadha was temporarily occupied by the Pālas. The reason of this sudden enterprise is not far to seek. During the long reign of Amoghavarṣa I, whose certain dates extend from 817 to 877 A.D., there was no war between the Gurjaras and the Rāṣṭrakūṭas.[4] In fact the only war between Bhoja I and the Rāṣṭrakūṭas was his war with the Rāṣṭrakūtas Dhruvarāja II of Gujarat some time before 867 A.D., in which Bhoja I himself was worsted.[5] After Bhoja I, Mahendrapāla succeeded to an empire which had reached its greatest extent at that time, from Punjab to the borders of Bengal, and from the foot of the Himalayas to Saurāṣṭra.[6] Mahendrapāla's reign was a very short one, as his certain dates range from 893 to 907 A.D. He had two wives and was succeeded by Bhoja II, his son by Dehanāgā.[7] Most probably there was some dispute about his succession, which may have been contested by his half-brother Mahīpāla II. Bhoja II was assisted to the throne by the Cedi Emperor Kokkalla I, which is referred to in the Bilhari inscription :—

Jitvā kṛtsnām yena pṛthvīm = apurvvaṅ-kīrtti-stambha-dvandvam = āropyate sma,
Kaumbhod-bhavyāndiśyasau Kṛṣṇarājaḥ Kaurveyāñ = ca Śrī-nidhir-Bhojadevaḥ— *verse* 17.[8]

We find a corroboration of this statement in the Benares grant of the Cedi Emperor Karṇadeva :—

Bhoje Vallabharāje Chitrakūṭa-bhūpāle,
Śaṅkaragaṇe ca rājani yasy = āsīd = abhayadaḥ pāṇīḥ—verse 7.[9]

---

1 J.R.A.S., 1910, pp. 150-51.
2 Cunningham, Arch. Surv. Rep., Vol. I, p. 36, pl. XIII. 1.
3 J A.S.B., N. S., Vol. IV, p. 105.
4 J.R.A.S., 1904, pp. 647-8.
5 Ind. Ant., Vol. XII, p. 181.
6 Epi. Ind., Vol. IX, p. 4.
7 Ind. Ant., Vol XV, p. 110.
8 Epi. Ind., Vol. I, p. 256.
9 Epi. Ind., Vol. II, p. 306,

So the Cedī Emperor also set up the Rāṣṭrakūṭa king Kṛṣṇa II, whose surname was Vallabharāja, on the throne of his father Amoghavarṣa I. Kṛṣṇa II defeated the Gurjaras and at the same time led an invasion into Bengal:—

Tasy = ottarjjita-Gurjaro hṛta-haṭa-llāṭ-odbhaṭa-śrīmado
Gauḍānāṁ vinaya-vratārppaṇa-gurus = Sāmudrā = nidrāharaḥ,
Dvārasth = Āṁga-Kaliṁga-Gāṁga-Magadhair = abhyarccit = ājñaś = ciraṁ sūnus = sūnṛtavāg = bhuvaḥ parivṛḍhaḥ Śrī Kṛṣṇarājo-bhavat.

-verse 13, Deoli plates of Kṛṣṇa III, and verse 15, Karhad plates of the same.[1]

The Gurjara king defeated by Kṛṣṇarāja II seems to be Bhoja II. He was succeeded very shortly by his half-brother Mahīpāla, under whom the area of the Gurjāra-Pratīhāra Empire became very circumscribed. The Rāṣṭrakūṭa king Kṛṣṇa II also had a very short reign and was succeeded by his grandson Indra III. His certain years range from 902 to 911, and as those of Bhoja II are almost the same, it is almost certain that he was the king who was defeated by Kṛṣṇa II. After the accession of Mahīpāla, whose certain dates range from 914 to 917, Indra III invaded the Gurjara Empire, crossed the Yamunā, occupied Kānyakubja, and most probably destroyed the city.[2] Mr. D. R. Bhandarkar has already proved that at that time Kṣitipāla or Mahīpāla was the reigning sovereign at Kanauj. In this campaign, Narasiṁha, a feudatory of Indra III, pursued the Gurjara king Mahīpāla as far as the confluence of the Ganges. Narasiṁha, according to the Karṇṇāṭaka-Śabdānuśāsana by Bhaṭṭa Kalaṅkadeva, "snatched from the Gurjara king's arms the goddess of victory, whom, though desirous of keeping, he had held too loosely. Mahīpāla fled as if struck by thunder-bolts, staying neither to eat nor rest, nor pick himself up, while Narasiṁha pursuing, bathed his horse at the junction of the Ganges and established his fame."[3] The mention of the confluence of the Ganges as the extremity of Narasiṁha's pursuit of Mahīpāla, without any mention of the Gauḍa king, most probably indicates that the Eastern frontier of the Gurjara-Pratīhāra Empire at that time extended up to the junction of the Ganges with the Sea. This is not to be wondered at as it is now certain that Magadha formed an integral part of the dominions of Mahīpāla's father Mahendrapāla. During this war Gopāla II of Bengal may have taken the opportunity of recovering some of the traditional possessions of his family and pushed the Western frontier as far as the eastern banks of the Sone This re-occupation of the Magadha may have been temporary. and Mahīpāla may have recovered the possession of his Eastern Provinces, with the help of the Candella Yaśovarmman[4] As no inscriptions of Gopāla's successor Vigrahapala II have been discovered, we are not in a position to say definitely whether Magadha continued to be a province of the Pāla Empire or was re-annexed by the Gurjaras. A MS. of the Pañcarakṣā written in the 26th year of Vīgrahapāladeva II is preserved in the British Museum collection : the latter part of its colophon runs thus :—

1 Ibid., Vol. V, p. 193; ibid., Vol. IV, p. 283.
2 Ibid., Vol. VII, p. 38.
3 Karnnataka-Sabdanusasana, ed. Lewis Rice, p. 26
4 Epi Ind., Vol. I, p. 122.

Parameśvara-Paramabhaṭṭāraka-Paramasaugata Mahārājādhirāja-Śrīmad-Vigrahapāladevasya pravardhamāna-vijayarājye-[about 15 indistinct akṣaras] Samvat 26 Āśāḍha dina 24 ||[1]

Before closing this chapter it should be noted that about this time an independent kingdom was established in Eastern Bengal. The existence of this kingdom was made known by the discovery of two copper-plate grants of Devakhaḍga, the last king of this dynasty. From these copper-plate grants it is now known that the dynasty reigned for three generations :—

Khaḍgodyama.
|
Jātakhaḍga.
|
Devakhaḍga.

Nothing is known about their dates save and except that the grants were issued in the thirteenth year of Devakhaḍga. The learned Editor of the plates has assigned them to the eighth or ninth century A.D.[2] But on comparison with the inscriptions of the Pāla Emperors it is found that their correct date would be the first half of the tenth century A.D. These two plates are the earliest inscriptions from Eastern Bengal proper, and the record next in order was incised so late as the reign of king Lakṣmaṇasena of Bengal.

---

1 Bendall, *Catalogue of the Sanskrit Manuscripts in the British Museum*, p. 232, J.R.A.S., 1910, p. 151.

2 Mem. A.S.B., Vol I, p. 86.

CHAPTER IV.

THE SECOND EMPIRE.

The period which follows is entirely different in character, the principal actors having changed. The great Gurjara-Pratīhāra Empire was rapidly dissolving and the Rāṣṭrakūṭa kings were gradually becoming weaker. Rāṣṭrakūṭa and Gurjara invasions became things of the past. New actors were appearing in the political arena. The invasion of the Great Coḷa Conqueror left a deep impression on north eastern India. It gave Bengal a new dynasty of kings and indirectly hastened the ruin of the Pāla Empire. After the Badal pillar inscription of Nārāyaṇapāla, there is no other inscription which can throw light on the history of Northern Bengal for three generations, i.e. till the time of Mahīpāla I. About this time some Mongolian tribes occupied the whole of the Northern Bengal and either massacred the old inhabitants or gradually forced them back southwards. A monolithic pillar now standing in the grounds of the place of the Mahārājas of Dinājpur bears a record of one of these Mongolian kings, who also claimed to be the lords of Gauḍa (*Gauḍeś-vara*). At present the whole of Northern Bengal is strewn over with pre-Muhammadan ruins and so far the general theory had been, that these temples, monasteries and towns were ruined at the time of the Muhammadan occupation of the country. But recently a plausible theory has been started by Mr. Ramā Prasād Canda, B.A., on the basis of Dinājpur pillar inscription, according to which the ruin of these ancient cities of Northern Bengal should be differently interpreted. The inscription on the Dinājpur pillar was brought to notice in 1871 when it was published with a rude lithograph.[1] The late Dr. Bloch examined the inscription during one of his tours and hastily gave a reading which I am afraid cannot be supported. Mr. Canda obtained some very clear and beautiful rubbings of this inscription during one of his many visits and submitted a paper on it to the Asiatic Society of Bengal.[2] According to Mr. Canda, the Koch, Mech and the Palias of the present day are the descendants of the Mongolians who invaded and settled in North Bengal during the latter half of the ninth and the tenth century A.D. The inscription on the Dinājpur pillar, which forms the basis of Mr. Canda's paper, records the erection of a temple of Śiva during the reign of a king of Gauḍa of the Kāmboja race, in the year 888 of some unspecified era. The date is expressed as a chronogram: *Kuñjara-Ghaṭā-varṣeṇa*, which probably means 888. This date cannot be referred to the Vikrama era as in that case it would be equivalent to 831 A.D., which is too early to suit the characters used in this inscription. Neither can it be referred to the

Kamboja or Mongolian invasion of North Bengal.

The date in the Dinājpur inscription.

---

1 Ind. Ant., Vol. I, pp. 127 and 227.

2 J.A.S.B., N.S, Vol. VII, p 619.

Gupta era as in that case it would be equal to 1207 A.D., which is certainly too late. The Kalacuri-Cedī era has never been found to have been used in Bengal. The Śaka era suits best though it has but been sparsely used in the North-East. In that case S. 888=966 A.D. falls just after the reign of Devapāla, the Pratihāra King of Kanauj. At that time the invaders must have settled down so that the invasion itself must have taken place some time earlier. Northern Bengal was in the undisputed possession of Nārāyaṇapāla at the time of the incision of Guravamiśra's record. So this invasion must have taken place some time between 850-950 A.D. The irruption of these Mongolian hordes must have taken place through the Himalayas, and most probably they were dispossessed of their former homes in the hills by some other invaders. So the Pālas after Nārāyaṇapāla, i.e. Rājyapāla, Gopāla II, and Vigrahapāla II, were having a rather bad time of it with the Gurjara Empire in the West and occasional Rāṣṭrakūṭa raids thrown in, and with Barbarian hordes advancing in untold numbers through the mountain passes of the North. No wonder that Magadha was annexed to the Gurjara-Pratīhāra Empire. At the time of the invasion of Indra III, the Eastern Frontier of the Gurjara-Pratīhāra Empire most probably extended right up to the modern Bhagirathi, and its confluence near Saugor Island. North Bengal must have remained in the possession of the Mongolian kings up to the end of the tenth century A.D. In the beginning of the eleventh century we find that the Pālas have recovered possession of Northern Bengal, and from this time onwards right up to the end of the second Pāla Empire, Northern Bengal continued to be in their possession. At the time of the Dinajpur inscription the Pālas seem to have been deprived of Gauḍa and consequently the Mongolian king became *Gauḍeśvara*. The name Kāmboja itself is of great interest. Thus far the Kāmbojas or Kamvojas were known to be a northern tribe who lived side by side with the Greeks in Afghanistan and the Western Punjab, as shown by the phrase "*Yona-Kāmbojesu*" in the XIII Rock Edict of Asoka.[1] The occurrence of the name in a Bengal inscription does not mean that the Kāmbojas, whole or part, immigrated into Bengal from the Punjab across the whole of Northern India, because that would have been an impossibility in those days, but shows that all Mongolians were called Kāmbojas, and that people with Mongolian features crossed over into Bengal through the Northern Mountains and as Kāmbojas. They may or may not have been a part of the people who became known during the Maurya period as the Kāmbojas.

Kāmboja kings of Gauḍa.

The occupation of Gauḍa by a barbarian tribe, at a time when the whole of Magadha was in the possession of the Gurjaras, shows that the kings of the Pāla dynasty between Nārāyaṇapāla and Vigrahapāla II and Mahīpāla I were kings in name only. Most probably they ruled over an insignficant kingdom surrounded by a large number of petty monarchies. The Tirumalai inscription of Rājendra Coḷa I shows that the ancient Gauḍa and Vaṅga had become divided into a large number of small kingdoms. The exact state and extent of the Pāla dominions under

[1] Epi Ind., Vol. II, p. 465.

Vigrahapāla are not known. Most probably he lost even what had belonged to Gopāla II as his son Mahīpāla I is said to have recovered his paternal kingdom. His only recorded war seems to have been conducted in Eastern Bengal. In the Āmgāchi and Dinājpur grants there is a verse about this :—

Deśe prāci pracura-payasi svaccham=āpīya toyaṁ svairaṁ bhrāntvā tad=anu malay-opatyakā-candaneṣu,

Kṛtvā sāndrais=taruṣu jaḍatāṁ śīkarair=abhra-tulyāḥ prāley-ādreḥ kaṭakam=abhajan yasya senā-gajendrāḥ.—verse 11 *Dinajpur grant of Mahīpāla.*[1]

But this is not very certain, as in the Amgāchi grant of Vigrahapāla the verse is attributed to Vigrahapāla III.[2]

After the death of Vigrahapāla II, Mahīpāla succeeded to what remained of the first Empire of the Pālas. In his Dinājpur grant he is said to have recovered the kingdom of his father :—

Hata-sakala-vipakṣaḥ saṅgare vāhu-darppād=anadhikṛta-viluptaṁ rājyam=āsādya pitryaṁ

Nihita-caraṇa-padmo bhūbhṛtāṁ murdhni tasmād=abhavad=avani-pālaḥ Śrī-Mahīpāladevaḥ.[3]

Mahīpāla I conquers Magadha

After the recovery of his paternal kingdom, Mahīpāla I must have turned his attention to the West. In his sixth year Nālanda was included in his kingdom as a manuscript copied at that place in that year of the king has been acquired for the Asiatic Society of Bengal by Mahāmahopādhyāya Hara Prasāda Śāstrī. Magadha seems to have continued in the possession of the king for a long time. In the eleventh year of the king an image of Buddha was dedicated in or near the temple of the Mahābodhi at Bodh-Gaya, and in the same year the great temple at Nālanda was restored, as it had been burnt down in a fire. After the conquest of Magadha, Mahīpāla seems to have attacked Tīrabhukti or Mithilā which continued in the possession of the king at least till his 48th year. His kingdom seems to have extended as far as Benares and continued to be included in it till 1020 A.D. In that year, two persons were deputed by the king, named Sthirapāla and Vasantapāla, to execute some repairs near the Buddhist city. The state of the Gurjara kingdom of Kanauj favoured the occupation. Only a few years before it had been devastated by Sultan Mahmūd of Ghazni, and after his departure, the king Rājyapāladeva had been deposed and murdered by the Indian Princes for having submitted to an alien conqueror. At that time Trilocanapāla was seated on the throne of the Gurjara-Pratīhāras and most probably his power did not extend beyond the confluence of the Yamunā.

and Mithilā.

Occupies Benares.

In spite of the victories during the earlier part of his reign, Mahīpāla I suffered some very severe reverses from the time of the rise of the Cedis, under Gāṅgeyadeva

[1] J.A.S.B., 1892, pp. 80 & 83.
[2] Ind. Ant., Vol. XXI, p. 101, and J A.S.B., 1892, p. 83, note 26.
[3] J.A.S.B., 1892, pp. 8—84, ll. 23-24

and Karṇadeva and the invasion of the Coḷa king Rājendra Coḷa I. The invasion of the Coḷa king took place before the 13th year of that prince, i.e. before 1025 A.D. Rājendra Coḷa earned the *viruda* of "*Gaṅgegoṇḍā*" or "Gangā-vijayī" by pushing as far North as the Ganges during this raid. The Tirumalai Rock inscription of the great conqueror records the Northern Campaign in detail. It is said that the king seized the "Oḍḍa-*viṣaya*" which was difficult to approach. This is clearly the Odra *Viṣaya* of the copper-plate inscriptions of Orissa. Then he entered "Koṣalaināḍu," i.e. the Kośala of the inscriptions of the Soma-vaṁśī kings of Orissa.[1] Next in order comes the subjugation of Daṇḍabhukti. The province has been identified by Mahāmahopādhyāya Hara Prasāda Śastri with the modern province of Bihar, because the ancient name of the town of Bihar was called Otantapuri by the Tibetans and Adwand Bihār by the Muhammadans. But this identification is scarcely tenable. The place is mentioned in the *Rāmacarita* of Sandhyākaranandi where a person named Jayasiṁha is said to have been its ruler and is said to have aided Rāmapāla in his wars in Northern Bengal. This man is said to have defeated Karṇa-Keśarī, the king of Orissa.[2] Most probably Daṇḍabhukti was the march-land between Orissa and Bengal, corresponding to the modern British districts of Midnapur and Balasore, and the man had defeated the king of Orissa in one of his expeditions against Bengal. It is more probable for a king of the march-lands to come into conflict with the king of Orissa than for the ruler of Magadha. Moreover the order in which the names of the countries are mentioned prevents us from supposing that Bihar is the country mentioned as we shall see later on. From Daṇḍabhukti the king passed on to Bengal, attacking and occupying the province of "Takkaṇa-Lāḍam." This name has been taken to be the equivalent of "Dakṣiṇa Lāṭa" by the late Dr. Kielhorn, which is the ancient name of Southern Gujarat.[3] But Messrs. Hultzsch and Venkayya take it to mean "Dakṣiṇa Virāṭa" or Southern Berar.[4] Mr. Venkayya is a great authority on Tamil, and he supposes that "the Tamil term "*Ilaḍa*" does not correspond to Sanskrit *Lāṭa* (Gujarat) but to *Virāṭa* (Berar)". But nowhere did it strike the learned scholars that the order in which the countries are mentioned, prevents us from supposing that either Berar or Gujarat is mentioned. In fact the country mentioned is Southern Rāḍhā. Mr. Venkayya will find, on re-considering the question, that *Dakṣiṇa-Rāḍhā* is a better equivalent for Tamil *Takkana-Lāḍam* than *Dakṣiṇa-Virāṭa*. Immediately after "Takkana-Lāḍam" we have the mention of *Vaṅgāla-deśa*, which all authorities agree as being equal to Vaṅga or Eastern Bengal. No sane man would turn from Orissa to conquer Southern Gujarat or Berar and then return to the East to conquer East Bengal,

Invasion of Rājendra Cola I.

Conquest of Odra and Kośala.

Daṇḍabukti and Southern Rāḍhā.

Uddandapura,

---

1 Epi Ind., Vol. III, p. 323

2 Mem. A.S.B., Vol. III, p. 36.

3 Epi. Ind., Vol. App. p. 120, No. 733. Vol. VIII. App. II, p. 22, No. 11.

4 Ann. Rep. on Epigraphy Madras, 1906-07, p. 87f.

after which he turns back to the West to defeat Mahīpāla in North Bengal and again rushes to North Gujarat or Berar to conquer it. The more natural explanation is that Rājendra Coḷa defeated Raṇaśūra, the ruler of Southern Rāḍhā, and then passed on through that country to invade Vaṅga. From very early times a part of Bengal has been called Rāḍhā. It occurs in a dated inscription of the Indo-Scythian period as Rārā. This inscription is at present in the Indian Museum, in Calcutta, but it was discovered in Mathurā in the United Provinces. The record mentions the erection of a Jaina image in the year 62 of the Kuṣana era = 150 A.D. at the request of a Jaina monk who was an inhabitant of the country of Rārā.[1] In comparatively modern times the name has been found on two copper-plate inscriptions :—

Rāḍhā as an ancient name.

(1) The newly discovered grant of the Sena king Vallālasena, found at Sitāhāṭi, near Kāṭwā, in the Burdwān district of Bengal, where we find that the village granted, Vāllahiṭṭi, was situated in the North Rāḍhā (*Uttara-Rāḍhā-maṇḍale*).[2] The very name Uttara-Rāḍhā occurs in the Tirumalai inscription as we shall see later on. Besides this, the kings of the Sena dynasty seem to have ruled in the Rāḍhā country :—

Vaṁśe tasy = ābhyudayini sadācāra-caryā-niruḍhi-prauḍhām
Rāḍhām-akalita-carair = bhūṣayantosnubhāvaiḥ,
Śaśvad = viśv-ābhaya-vitaraṇa-sthūla-lakṣyāvalakṣaiḥ kīrtty-ullolaiḥ snapita-viyato jajñire rājaputrāḥ.—verse 3.[3]

There being a Uttara-Rāḍhā we can say from immediate inference, that there was a Dakṣina-Rāḍhā, which in Tāmil becomes "Takkana-Lāḍam."

(2) Besides this the Kenduāpatna plates of Narasiṁhadeva II of Orissa, dated Śaka 1217 = 1296 A.D., show very clearly that Rāḍhā and Vārendrī were well-known names of divisions of Bengal :—

Rāḍhā-Vārendra-yavanī-nayan-āñjan-āśru-pūreṇa dūra-viniveśitakālima-śrīḥ,
Tad-vipralambha-karaṇ-ādbhuta-nistaraṅgā Gaṅgāpi nūnam-amunā Yamun = ādhun = ābhūt.—verse 84.[4]

At the time of the Coḷa invasion a king named Raṇaśūra was ruling Southern Rāḍhā. In Bengal there is a tradition that a dynasty of kings with the affix Śūra ruled in Bengal before the Pālas. We have no reliable evidence for this. But three kings of this family, at least with the word Śūra affixed to their names, have been mentioned in epigraphs. These are: Raṇaśūra, of the Tirumalai inscription; Lakṣmīśūra, a king of a division of Bengal named Apara-Mandāra, a contemporary of Rāmapāla, who was the headman of all feudatories of Forest lands (*samastāṭavika-sāmanta-cakra-cuḍāmaṇiḥ*); a man named Damaśūra, who is mentioned in a newly-discovered inscription of the time of Gopāla III, found at Manda in the Rājshāhi district of Bengal. After conquering Southern Rāḍhā, the Coḷa king did not proceed to subdue the northern portion of it, but on the other hand, passed eastwards towards Vaṅga,

1 J.A.S.B., N.S., Vol. V, p. 239.
2 Vaṅgiya Sāhitya Parishad Patrikā, Vol. XVII, p. 235.
3 Ibid., p. 235.
4 J.A.S.B., Vol. LXV, 1895, p. 250.

which was then ruled by a king named Govinda-Candra. This king has been wrongly identified with a king named Govinda-Candra or Govi-Canda, about whom some songs are current in the State of Kuch-Bihar and the Rungpur district of Bengal. The king of that name mentioned in the Tirumalai inscription is expressly stated to be the King of Eastern Bengal, and so there is very little chance of identifying him with the local hero of Rungpur. After conquering Eastern Bengal, Rājendra Coḷa turned towards the West and faced Mahīpāla, who had been rightly identified by the late Dr. Kielhorn with the Pāla king Mahīpāla I, who was defeated. The inscription is so worded that one at once understands that by defeating Mahīpāla, the king was able to reach "*Uttira-Lāḍam*" and the Ganges. *Uttira-Lāḍam* for the same reasons as have been stated above in the case "*Takkana-Lāḍam*" should be taken to be Northern Rāḍhā, which is actually mentioned as a maṇḍala in the Sītāhāṭi grant of Vallālasena Moreover there is no evidence to prove that Berar or Virāṭa was divided into two parts at any time. Again from Bengal Rājendra Coḷa reached Uttara-Rāḍha and after that the Ganges. It is a far cry from Berar to the Ganges, but the sacred river which added lustre to the conquest of Rājendra Coḷa I in the eyes of the Southern people actually forms the Northern boundary of Rāḍha. The divisions of Bengal across the great river are known as Mithilā and Vārendra, the latter of which is mentioned in the Rāma-carita,[1] and at least three copper-plates. So now it is clear that the Ganges formed the Northern boundary of the conquest of Rajendra Coḷa I. Curiously enough he did not attempt to cross the Ganges to the other side. The Tirumalai inscription being a *Praśasti* does not mention such details. But the desired details are supplied by an ancient manuscript discovered by Mahāmahopādhyāya Hara Prasāda Śāstrī and now in the library of the Asiatic Society of Bengal. In 1893 the Mahāmahopādhyāya published notes on a find of ancient Sanskrit manuscripts among which was a drama named Caṇḍa-Kauśika, by Ārya Kṣemīśvara. This play was enacted before the king by his order, and it contains a verse in which the king Mahīpāla I is compared with Candragupta and a people named Karṇāṭakas, to the Nandas. So this contemporary work gives the credit of defeating the Karṇāṭakas to Mahīpāla I. The Karṅāṭakas seem to be the southerners who invaded Bengal under Rājendra Coḷa I. It appears that though Mahīpāla I was defeated by Rājendra Coḷa when he crossed into Rāḍhā from East Bengal, he prevented him from crossing the Ganges into Varendra or Northern Bengal, and so the Coḷa conqueror had to turn back from the banks of the Ganges. The manuscript on which Mahāmahopādhyāya Hara Prasāda Śāstrī relies is not a modern one, as it was copied in 1331 A.D[2] The invasion of the Coḷa king did not change the political divisions of the country, but it left one permanent mark in the shape of a body of settlers, who occupied the thrones of Bengal and Mithilā as the Sena and Karṇāta dynasties during the latter days of the Pālas.

Conquest of Eastern Bengal.

Defeat of Mahīpāla and conquest of Northern Rādha.

The Coḷa invasion took place, as has been stated above, before the thirteenth

[1] Mem. A.S.B., Vol. III, p. 55.

[2] J.A.S.B., Vol. LXII, 1893, p. 250.

year of the king, i.e. 1025 A.D. The very next year we find that the Wheel of Law at Benares is being repaired, and a new temple (*Gandha-kūṭī*) built by the brothers Sthirapāla and Vasantapāla under the orders of the king.

The record of these events is found in an inscription discovered amidst the ruins of Sārnāth near Benares more than a hundred years ago.[1] It is incised on the pedestal of an image of Buddha, which is at present in the Provincial Museum at Lucknow. This image was dedicated in the Vikrama year 1083=1026 A.D. Very soon after this Benares was taken away from the Pālas by the Cedī Emperor of Gāṅgeyadeva who invaded North-Eastern India about this time and had occupied it six or seven years ago. Some time before 1881 A.D., some metal images were found near a village Imādpur in the Muzaffarpur district of Bengal,[2] which were pronounced by Dr. Hoernle to have been dedicated in the 48th year of Mahīpāladeva.[3] As these images were found in Tirhut or Tīrabhukti, it is natural to conclude that Mithila was in the possession of the Pālas up to the 48th year of Mahīpāla I. But six years before the erection of the temple of Sārnath, Mithilā passed out of the hands of the Pālas. In the year 1020 A.D. Gāṅgeyadeva was in possession of Tīrabhukti or Mithilā. A copy of the Rāmāyaṇa copied in that year V. S. 1076 mentions Tīrabhukti as being in the possession of Gāṅgeyadeva:—

The struggle with the Cedi Empire.

Conquest of Mithilā.

Saṁvat 1076 āṣāḍha badi 4 mahārājādhirāja puṇyāvaloka-somavaṁśodbhava-Gauḍadhvaja-Śrīmad-Gāṅgeyadeva-bhujyamāṇa Tīrabhuktau kalyāṇavijayarājye.[4]

Very soon after Benares passed into the hands of the Cedīs. Karṇṇadeva, the son of Gāṅgeyadeva, was in possession of Benares in 1042 A.D. (Kalacurī-Cedī year 793).[5] Tīrabhukti or Mithilā was never recovered by the Pālas. The only Pāla records referring to this Province are the Bhāgalpur grant of Nārāyāṇapāla and the Imādpur image inscription of Mahīpāla I.

Mahīpāla I was succeeded by his son Nayapāla, who is called Nyāyapala on the authority of some unpublished record, by Mahāmahopādhyāya Hara Prasāda Śastrī. According to Tārānātha, Mahīpāla reigned for fifty-two years, which is most probably correct as the Imādpur images were dedicated in the 48th year of the king. Of the relations of the king we only know the names of the brothers Sthirapāla and Vasantapāla, who were most probably nearly related to him besides his son Nayapāla. The long reign of Mahīpāla I is very fruitful in inscription and manuscript records. The earliest of these is the manuscript of Aṣṭasāhasrikā Prajñāpāramitā, now in the University Library at Cambridge. The colophon runs thus :—

Successor and length of reign

Parameśvara paramabhaṭṭāraka-paramasaugata-mahārājādhirāja Śrīman-Mahīpāladeva pravarddhamāna-vijayarājye samvat 5 Āśvine Kṛṣṇe.[6]

1 As. Res., Vol. IX, p. 204. 2 Proc. A.S.B., 1881, p. 98. 3 Ind. Ant., Vol. XIV, p. 165, note 17.
4 Cat of Sans. MSS. in the Durbar Liby., Nepal. Hist. Intro., p. 18, and No. 1079 (kha), p. 34.
5 Epi. Ind., Vol. II, p. 300.
6 Bendall's Cat. of Buddhist Sans. MSS. in the Univ. Liby., Cambridge, p. 101.

The date next in order is to be found in a manuscript of the same work, collected by Mahāmahopādhyāya Hara Prasāda Śāstrī, for the Asiatic Society of Bengal. The reading of the colophon as revised by the late Dr. Theodor Bloch runs as follows:—

Deyadharmmeyaṁ pravaramahāyānayāyinaḥ Tāḍivāḍi-Mahāvihārīya āvasthitena Śākyācārya-sthavira-Sādhuguptasya yad = atra puṇyan = tad = bhavatv = ācāry = opādhyāya-mātā-pitṛ-purangamaṁ kṛtvā sakala-satva-rāśer = anuttara-jñāna phal = āvāptaya iti. Paramabhaṭṭāraka-Mahārājādhirāja-Parameśvara-Paramasaugata Śrīmad-Vigrahapāladeva-pādānudhyāta Paramabhaṭṭāraka-Mahārājādhirāja-Parameśvara-Paramasaugata Śrīman=Mahīpāladeva-pravarddhamāna-Kalyāṇavijayarājye ṣaṣṭha-saṃbatsare abhilikhyamāne yatrāṅke samvat 6 Kārttika-Kṛṣṇa-trayodaśyān = tithau maṅgalavāreṇa bhaṭṭārikā-niṣpāditam=iti || Śrī Nālandāvasthita-Kalyāṇamitra-Cintāmaṇikasya likhita iti.[1]

This colophon proves that in the sixth year of Mahīpāla Nālanda was in his possession, and thus a part at least of Magadha was included in his dominions. Next in order comes an inscription incised on the pedestal of an image of Buddha, in the attitude of touching the earth (*Bhūmisparśa mudrā*). This image is now being worshipped as one of the five Pāṇḍus, in a small shrine just in front of the entrance of the great temple at Bodh-Gayā. The inscription consists of three lines, in an imperfect state of preservation, the first part of each line having lost a number of letters. It is dated in the eleventh year of the reign of Mahīpāla, presumably the first, as the letters still show signs of acute angles at their lower extremities. It has been referred to by Cunningham.[2] The text runs :—

1. *Deya-dharmmoyam .... tad-bhavatv=ācāry=opādhāya-mātā-pitṛ-pūrvvaṅgamaṁ kṛtvā sakala-satva-rāśer=anuttara-jñān=āvāptaya-iti ॥ Mahā-*
2. *[rājādhirāja-Parameśvara-Pa]ramabhaṭṭāraka-Paramasaugata-Śrī-mān=Mahīpāladeva-pravarddhamāna-vijayarājye ekādaśame samvatsare abhilikhya[māne]*
3. *.......... pañcamyān=tithau gandha-Kūṭī-dvaya-sahitā......karitāv=iti.*

The name of the donor of the two temples (*Gandha-Kūṭīdvaya*) and the image is unfortunately lost. As the name of the month in this inscription is illegible it is impossible to state whether it was incised before or after Balāditya's Nālandā inscription of the same year which has been placed next in order. This inscription was discovered by Broadley among the ruins of the great Vihāra at Nālandā where it was found on a door-jamb. According to this inscription the great temple at Nālandā was restored after being burnt down by a man named Bālāditya, a Jyāvisa of Teläḍhaka (modern Telara) who had emigrated from Kauśāmbī, in the eleventh year of Mahīpāladeva.[3]

The restoration of the Great Vihāra at Nālandā.

---

[1] Proc. A.S.B., 1899, p. 69. [2] Cunningham, Arch. Surv. Rep., Vol. III, p. 122, No. 9, pl. XXXVII, No. 5.
[3] J.A.S.B., Vol. IV, p. 106. No. IV, pl. VI.

The conquest of Northern Bengal must have taken place some years earlier. In his ninth year Mahīpāla granted the village of Kuraṭapallikā, with the exception of Cuṭapallikā, in the Gokalikā *maṇḍala*, Koṭivarṣa *viṣaya* of the Pauṇḍravarddhana *bhukti* to a Brāhmaṇa named Kṛṣṇādityaśarmaṇ. It has been proved by another inscription, the Maṇahali grant of Madanapāla, that the Koṭivarṣa *viṣaya* was situated in Northern Bengal, as both inscriptions have been discovered in the Dinājpur district.[1] An inscription incised on the pedestal of a colossal image of Buddha, still in situ, at Tetrawan, an ancient site six miles from Bihār in the Patna District of Bengal, contains the name of Mahīpāla, the rest having become illegible.[2] Most probably it was dedicated during the reign of Mahipāladeva. The images discovered at Imādpur in the Muzaffarpur district of Bengal in 1881 were most probably dedicated in the 48th year of Mahīpāla I,[3] as Mahīpāla II had a very short reign. The 48th year of Mahīpāla I must have fallen before 1020 A.D., as in that year the Cedi Emperor Gāṅgeyadeva was in possession of Tīrabhukti or Tirhut. The last inscription of Mahīpāla is the Sarnath inscription of the Vikrama year 1083. This inscription was either posthumous, or incised when the city of Benares had passed from the hands of the Pālas to those of the Cedis. The repair of the Wheel of Law and the building of the temple seem to have begun some time before and the work was completed either after Mahīpāla's death or in his last year, when he had lost Benares and Tirhut. Mahīpāla was succeeded by his son Nayapāla, called Nyāyapāla by Mahāmahopādhyāya Hara Praśāda Śāstri, on some unknown authority. His minister's name was Vāmaṇabhaṭṭa, who is the Dūtaka of the Bangarh grant of this king called the Dinājpur grant by Dr. Kielhorn.

Nayapāla Acc. 1025—30 A.D.

Nayapāla succeeded the throne of the Pālas some time between 1025—30 A.D. At that time the extent of the Pāla Empire had been considerably diminished by the loss of Benares and Tīrabhukti. Gāṅgeyadeva was succeeded by his son Karṇa, who with the help of some Southerners overran the whole of Northern India. The Nāgpur praśasti of Udayāditya of Mālava speaks of him as one who, joined by the Karṇāṭakas, had swept over the earth like a mighty ocean :—

Tasmin=vāsava-vandhutām=upagate rājye ca kuly=ākule
Magnasvāmini tasya vandhur=Udayādityo-bhavad-bhūpatiḥ
Yen=oddhṛitya mahārṇṇav=opama-milat=Karṇṇāṭa-Karṇṇa-prabhum=urvvīpālakadarthitāṁ bhuvam=imāṁ Śrīmad-Varāhāyitaṁ—verse 32.[4]

According to the Bheraghat inscription of Alhaṇadevī, we find:—

Pāṇḍyaś=caṇḍimatām=mumoca Muralas=tatyāja garvva-grahaṁ
Kuṅgaḥ sadgatim=ājagāma cakape Vaṅgaḥ Kaliṅgaiḥ saha,
Kīra Kīravadāsa pañjaragṛhe Hūṇaḥ praharṣaṁ jahau
Yasmin=rājani Śaurya-bibhrama-bharaṁ vibhraty-apūrvva-prabhe—verse 12.[5]

---

1 Ibid, 1893, pt. I, p. 77.
2 Arch. Surv. Rep., Vol. III, p. 123.
3 Ind. Ant., Vol. XIV, p. 105, note 17.
4 Epi. Ind, Vol. II, p. 185.
5 Ibid., p. 11.

Karṇṇadeva is said to have subdued or held in check the Pāṇḍyas, Muralas, Kuṅgas, Vaṅgas, Kaliṅgas, Kiras and Hūṇas. In the Karanbel inscription of Jayasiṁhadeva it is stated that Karṇṇa was waited upon by the Coḍa, Kuṅga, Hūṇa, Gauḍa, Gurjara and Kīra princes:—

Nīcaiḥ sañcara Coḍa-Kuṅga kim=idaṁ phalgu tvayā valgyate Hūṇ=aivam raṇituṁ na yuktam=iha te tvaṁ Gauḍa garvvan=tyaja,

m=aivaṁ Gurjjara garjja Kīra nibhṛto varttasva sevā-gatān=itthaṁ yasya mitho-virodhi-nṛpatīn dvāstho vininye janaḥ.—L. 11—12.[1]

According to the Cedi inscriptions Karṇṇa subdued or defeated the king of Gauḍa, whoever he might be. Mr. Monmohan Cakravartti first of all pointed out mentions of a war between Nayapāla and the king of Karṇya. The term "king of Karṇya" seems to be a translation of the Sanskrit word "Karṇarāja," "the king Karṇa." The form Karṇya seems to be a mistake.[2] In his article on the Kṛṣṇadvārika temple inscription of Nayapāla Mr. Cakravartti has pointed out that Atīśa mediated between Nayapāla and the king of Karṇya about the year 1035 A.D. So the Cedi Emperor Karṇadeva, who is in reality the same person as the king of Karṇya of Tibetan literature, must have invaded Magadha some time before 1035 A.D.[3] The incidents of the campaign are mentioned in Rai Śarat Candra Dās Bahadur's article on the Life of Atīśa:—

Karṇadeva, the Cedī, invades Magadha.

"During Atīśa's residence at Vajrasena a dispute having risen between the two, Nayapāla, king of Magadha, and the Tirthika, king of Karṇya of the West, the latter made war upon Magadha. Failing to capture the city, his troops sacked some of the sacred Buddhist institutions and killed altogether five (men) .... Afterwards when victory turned towards (Nayapāla) and the troops of Karṇya were being slaughtered by the armies of Magadha, he took the king of Karṇya and his men under his protection and sent them away............ Atīśa caused a treaty to be concluded between the two kings. With the exception of the articles of food that were destroyed at the time of war, all other things which had fallen in the hands of the parties were either restored or compensated for".[4]

Nayapāla must have reigned at least fifteen years as two of his inscriptions were incised in that year. The first is the Kṛṣṇa-dvārikā temple inscription, referred to above, which records the erection of a temple of Viṣṇu by a low class Brāhmaṇa named Viśvāditya, the son of Śūdraka and the grandson of Paritoṣa, in the fifteenth year of king Nayapāladeva. The verses were composed by a veterinary named Sahadeva and the engraving was done by the artisan Saṭṭasoma, son of Adhipasoma. The second inscription was discovered by Mr. Parameśvar Dayāl, then Court of Wards Head Clerk in Gayā, in 1884, inside the small temple of Narasiṁha in the Viṣṇupāda compound. It was pointed out by him to Mr. Cakravartti,[5] and to the late Dr.

Length of reign, Inscriptions and MS. Records.

[1] Ind. Ant., Vol. XVIII, p. 217.

[2] Jl. Bud. Text Soc., Vol. I, p. 9.

[3] J.A.S.B., 1900, pt. I, p. 192.

[4] Jl. Bud. Text Soc., Vol. I, p. 9, note.

[5] J.A.S.B, 1900, pt. I, p. 191, note 1.

Bloch in 1902.[1] But as this inscription has never been properly edited I am taking this opportunity of transcribing it :—

(1) *Oṁ Lakṣmīś=ciraṅ=jayati vāri-nidher-aneka-manthā-kulād-adhigatā puruṣottamasya* । *Suihyat=tirovalita-sammada ghūrṇṇamāna-netrāvalokana nirasta-samasta vighnā* ॥

(2) *S=eyaṁ vrahmapurī Gay=eti jagati khyātā svayaṁ vedhasā sthātuṁ brahmavidāṁ pur=īva ghaṭitā mokṣasya saukhyasya ca* । *vrumaḥ kiñ=ca bhavanti yatra pitaraḥ pretā-*

(3) *-layāvāsinaḥ pādaspṛṣṭa-jala-pradāna-vidhinā nāk=āṅganā-nāyakāḥ* ॥ *Asyām vabhūva puri vakragati-dvijihva-samrāḍ-bhujaṅga-ripur-acyuta-pādasevī* । *yo*

(4) *nāma viṣṇur-rathavad*[2]*-dvijarājavaryaḥ prītyā satāṁ ca Paritoṣa iti prasiddhaḥ* ॥ *Tasmād=vidher=iva vabhūva sanatkumāraḥ Śrī Śūdrako vimala-vuddir=anekavidyaḥ* ।

(5) *Bhūy-opi yena vidhin=aiva kṛtā Gay=eyaṁ vāhvor-valena suciraṁ paripālitā ca* ॥ *Tasmād=ajāyata sutaḥ sutavad=dvijānāṁ yo-bhūt suvismaya-rasāvaha-kartaka-.*[3]

(6) *ś=ca* ॥ *Viśvāpakāraka-nirākṛtaye-vatīrṇṇaḥ Śrī Viśvarūpa iti kīrttita viśvarūpaḥ* ॥ *Yaṁ prāpya c=ārthijana-vṛndam-akalpa-dānam=āpurbhavat*[4] *pulaka-jālam—ana-*

(7) *-nta-modam* । *Sphīti-sphurad=dhana-kṛtārthatayā durāpa-cintāmaṇi-grahaṇakaṁ na kadāpi dadhmau* ॥ *Yen=āsurāri-caritena mahodayena yantī rasātalam-ivāvani-*

(8) *-r=uddhṛt-eyaṁ . Śrī-mad-Gayā-kali-mala-dvija-rāja-pakṣa-saṁkṣobha-kampita-tanur=bhuja-vikrameṇa* ॥ *Yasmai viśuddha-caritāya nisagra*[5]*-sauryarāśi-priyāya vi-*

(9) *-nay-āmala-bhūṣaṇāya āvālyataḥ prabhṛti deva-manuṣya-loko vaddhāñjaliś=cirataraṁ spṛhayāṁ cakāra* ॥ *Ten=emāñ=ca GADĀDHAR=ĀDI-nilayavyājena tāḥ kī-*[6]

(10) *kīrttayaḥ svetanśor=iva raśmayaḥ sughaṭitā[ḥ] santāpa-śāntyai sadā Yatrāmbhonidhi vīcivad=daśadiśām prakṣālan-aikacchaṭāḥ pātāla-prativāsi-ghora-timi-*

(11) *-ra-pradhvansa-dīpā iva* ॥ *Etāḥ santu Gayāpurī sutaruṇī bhūṣāvalī kīrttayo yāvac=candra-divākarau ca gaganaṁ Śri-viśvarūp-āhvay..ḥ Kartāsāṁ ca tathā pu-*

(12) *-rāṇa-puruṣān rājño-pi dhikkṛtya sad-yen-ākasmika-vismay-aika-rasiko loko muhur=murcchitaḥ* । *Dākṣiṇyād=uparuddhena prītis-timita cetasā* । *Praśastir-e-*

(13) *-ṣā vihitā VAIDYA ŚRĪ-VAJRAPAṆINĀ* । *Vijñāna-kauśal-ollāsa-jāta-naipuṇa karmmaṇā . praśastir = eṣā likhitā Sarvvānandena dhīmatā* । *Kṣīrāmbho-nidhi- mekha-*

(14) *-lā-maṇi-guṇ-ālaṁkāritāyā bhuvo bharttuḥ ŚRI-NAYAPĀLA-DEVA-nṛpate rājñāśrīyaṁ vibhrataḥ saṁvṛtte tarasaiva PAÑCA-DAŚAME RĀJYASYA SAMVATSARE kīrttiḥ siddhim = upāgatā bhagavataḥ*

(15) *Śrī-mad-GADĀDHĀRIṆAḤ* ।

---

[1] Proc. A.S.B., 1902, pp. 66-67.
[2] *va* added afterwards.
[3] Or—Kautaka—
[4] Read—manalpa-dānam = āvirbhavat—
[5] Read nisarga—
[6] The last syllable of this line is superfluous.

The main object of the inscription seems to be the recording of the ancestry and the name of the donor as well as the date of the building of the Temple of Gadādhara and several other minor temples of Viṣṇu. As the inscription itself was found in the temple of Narasiṁha which is only few paces behind that of Gadādhara at Gayā it seems certain that the ancient materials which have been profusely used in the modern temple of Gadādhara are the remains of the temple built by Viśvarūpa in the fifteenth year of the reign of Nayapāladeva.

The Kṛṣṇa-Dvārikā temple inscription referred to above also records the erection of temple of Viṣṇu in the fifteenth year of Nayapāla :—

Saptāmvu-rāśi-visarat (ac-ch) ślatha mekhalāyā asyā bhūvaḥ kati na bhūmi-bhujo-vabhūvuḥ,

Siddhiṁ na kasyacid=agād=yad=analpa-kalpais=ten=ātra Kīrttanam=akāri Janārdanasya,—verse 17.[1]

The modern temple of Kṛṣṇa-dvārikā is built almost entirely of ancient materials and it is quite possible that these materials are the only remnants of Viśvāditya or Viśvarūpa's temple. The only other existing record of Nayapāla is in the colophon of a manuscript of Pañca-rakṣā in the collection of the Cambridge University :—

Deyadharmosyam = pravara-mahāyāna-yāyinyāḥ Paramopāsikā-Rājñī-Uddākāyā yad=atra puṇyan=tad=bhavatv=ācāry=opādhyāya-matā-pitṛ (pūrvaṅgama) ṅ-kṛtvā sakala-satva-rāśer-anuttara-jñān=āvāptaya iti || Paramasaugata-Mahārājādhirāja-Parameśvara Śrī-man=Nayapāladeva-pravarddhamāna-vijayarājye samvat 14 Caitra dine 27 likhit-eyaṁ bhaṭṭārikā iti.[2]

Nothing else is known about Nayapāla and his relations. He was succeeded by his son Vigrahapāla III. Nayapāla's reign most probably did not extend beyond the date of the Kṛṣṇa-dvārikā and Gadādhara temple inscriptions and seems to have come to an end some time between 1045 and 1050 A.D. It is said in a commentary on Cakradatta that Cakrapāṇi Datta was the kitchen superintendent of king Nayapāla.[3]

Vigrahapāla III : his war.

At the beginning of his reign Vigrahapāla came into conflict with his father's antagonist, the Cedi Emperor Karṇa. Karṇa's power at that time was at its lowest ebb. He was being constantly defeated by the neighbouring princes. He had a very long reign, his own with that of his son having covered a century. In the height of his power he had overrun the whole of Northern India but in his old age he suffered many reverses. He was defeated by the Candella Kīrttivarmaṇ,[4] by Udayāditya of Mālava,[5] by Bhīmadeva I of Anahilvād, who is eulogised by the grammarian Hema-candra for having defeated Karṇa in battle,[6] and by the Western Cālukya Someśvara I, which is recorded by the poet

1 J.A.S.B., 1900, pt. I, p. 184.

2 Bendall's Cat. Skt. MSS. in the Univy. Liby., Cambridge, p. 175. No. 1688.

3 Cakrapāṇi, Ed by Śivadāsa Sena, Calcutta, B. S. 1302, p. 407.

4 Epi. Ind., Vol. I, pp. 220, 326, 130, 132.

5 Ibid., Vol. II, p. 192.

6 Bühler— Über das Leben des Jaina Monchs Hema—Chandra, p. 69.

Bilhaṇa in his *Vikramāṇka-deva Carita*, where Karṇa is mentioned as the god of death to the Lord of the Kalañjara mountains, e.g. the Caṇḍellas.[1] In his last war with the Pālas, Karṇa was defeated and sued for peace. Vigrahapāla III married the aged king's daughter Yauvanaśrī. Karṇa's war with Vigrahapāla and his subsequent relationship was made known to us by Mahāmahopādhyāya Hara Prasāda Śāstrī's unique discovery, "The Rāmacarita of Sandhyākaranandi":—

Marriage with Princess Yauvanaśrī, the daughter of Karṇa.

Anyatra | yo Vigrahapālo Yauvanaśriyā Karṇasya rājñaḥ sutayā saha Kṣauṇīmudūḍhavān । Sahasā valen-āvito-rakṣito raṇajitaḥ saṅgrāmajitaḥ Karṇo Dāhal=ādhipatir=yena । Raṇajita eva parantu rakṣito na unmūlitaḥ—Commentary on verse 9.[2]

It is evident from the commentary the Karṇa suffered a severe reverse at the hands of his future son-in-law and that though defeated he was not "uprooted," i.e. deprived of his kingdom. It may be that the proud Cedī gave his daughter to Vigrahapāla to avert a calamity. Vigrahapāla III probably had a very short reign, not exceeding thirteen years. Had he lived longer the Pāla Empire may have lasted for some time. His sons were continually quarrelling among themselves and reigned for very short periods. The subordinate princes eagerly availed themselves of the opportunity of throwing off the yoke and the Pāla princes never gained the opportunity of subjugating the territories lost at this time.

Three inscriptions of Vigrahapāla III have been discovered as yet, of which one is on a copper-plate and the other two on stone. The copper-plate is the well-known one from Āmgachi in the Dinājpur District. The inscription has been edited many times but the first twenty lines edited by the late Prof. Kielhorn[3] and the remaining portion by Dr. A. F. R. Hoernle[4] are the only reliable versions. A fresh edition of this important inscription is very urgently wanted I hope to take up this work ere long and compare it with the Bangarh grant of Mahīpāla I as suggested by Mr. V. A. Smith.[5] The Āmgāchi plate records the grant of half of the village named Brāhmaṇī in the Koṭivarṣa viṣaya of the Pauṇḍravarddhana bhukti to a Brāhmaṇa named Khoddhata-devaśarmaṇ on the ninth day of Caitra in the 13th year of the king.[6] On the other two inscriptions of this king, the Akṣayavaṭa inscription is the most important. It was noticed by Cunningham in the third volume of his Reports. The late Dr. Th. Bloch published a summary of its contents but at that time the last lines of the inscription were covered with plaster and so he missed the name of the king and the date. After frequent trials I succeeded in removing the plaster and copying the entire inscription. The central part of the inscription has suffered seriously and is only partly legible. Otherwise the inscription is quite clear. It records the erection of a liṅga (Vaṭeśa) at Akṣayavaṭa and another called Prapitā-

---

1 Vikramanka deva-carita, I, 102 3, XVIII, 93.

2 Mem. A.S.B., Vol. III, p. 22.

3 Ind. Ant., Vol. XXI, p. 97.

4 Ibid , Vol. XIV, p. 166.

5 Ibid., Vol. XXXVIII, p. 240.

6 Ibid., Vol. XIV, p. 168.

maheśvara close by, in the fifth year of the reign of Vigrahapāladeva. As the record has never been properly edited before I do so from the original stone :—

(1) *Oṁ Oṁ namaḥ Śivāya* || *Dayābhāṇḍāgāraṁ niravadhi-jagad-doṣa-vijayi sphuraj=jñāna-jyotiḥ prasara-nihata-dhvānta-nicayaṁ* | *Kim-apy-antaḥ sāntaṁ sahaja-sukha-pīyuṣa-laharī......*

(2) *-ra hṛdayamaṅgho haratu vaḥ* || *Āsandhāyā-kalaṅkān=prati-vapuṣa iva brāhmaṇān=avja-janmā svargga-dvār-ādhirohām=amṛta-pada-sukha-prāptaye pretya bhājaḥ* | *Sākṣāt saṁsāra-bhūṣāva........*

(3) *Śrīmad-bhūmiṁ śaśvat=trailokya-lakṣmī=nilayam=iva purīṁ Śrī Gayām=eṣa cakre* || *Gayāyām=etasyāṁ puri sakala-saundarya nilaye dvijātīnāṁ mānyo dvija-pada-sarojāka......*

(4) *-ma premnā parama-paritoṣasya jananād=abhūd=dhanyaḥ Śrīmān sı khalu Paritoṣ-āhvaya iti* || *Tasmād=abhūj=jalanidhır=iva śītaraśmiḥ Śrī Śūdrako vimalakāntir=ananta-lakṣmī* [*ḥ*] ......

(5) *kaṇṭha-sravābhirāmam=ānanditāni yaśasā bhuvan-āntarani* || *Āsādy=āmara-rāja-rājya-padavīṁ devībhir=ākrīḍitaṁ divy-ātmatvam=anaṅga-darppa-dalan =odgār-aika-modaṁ vapu* [*ḥ ......*

(6) *-nti* (?) *kautuka-rasān=marttyo' vatīrṇṇas-tato jāto deva-kumāra-murttirasamaḥ Śrī Viśvarūp=āhvayaḥ* || *Yo vidhvasta-samasta-vairi-nivahaḥ sphuryat= pratāp-ānalaḥ saujanyasya nidāna......*

(7) *-ma keli-drumaḥ* | *sāndrānandamayo nisargga-madhura-vyāhāra-ratnākaro dīn= ānātha-vipanna-cāraṇa-gaṇa-trāṇāya cintāmaṇiḥ* || *Gaṇḍasthale mṛgamad-āmala-patra-bhaṅgān svairaṁ......*

(8) *-lekhanībhīḥ* | *Adyāpi yasya sura-kinnara-gīyamānāṁ devyaḥ śilāsu vijaya-stutim=ālikhanti* || *Dharmmeṇ=otsvasitaṁ mudā vihasitaṁ saṁloka maryā-dayā trayyā visphuritaṁ......*

(9) *-ttribhir-jjṛmbhitaṁ* | *yasmin-āsvāmini sarvvataḥ samudaye tepy-arthinaḥ sāhasaṁ sāndrānandamayāḥ sva-dainya-virahān-nṛtyanti pūrṇṇāśayāḥ* || *N=occaiś-caṇḍa-karo na c=āpi vigata......*

(10) *ten-āstam yāti ja lātmabhiḥ pratihato n-ānyair=apūrṇṇo bhavaḥ* | *Jihvāgreṇa vināgasaḥ prati muhūrtt-āpya sthirān-agrahīn-naivāsaṁga-digamvar-aika nirato yo viśvarūpaḥ..*||......

(11) *-marādhipo pi cakito Vrahmāpi yad-vismito devo Viṣṇurapi sphuṭaṁ vihasito Rudropi romāñcitaḥ* | *Uddāma-prasarat-prasanna-vahule yat-kīrtti-kallolinī -gambhīr-āmbhasi majja......*

(12) *-pi saṁvodhita* || *Yad=durggamaṁ sarati dūrataraṁ durāpaṁ yac=cetasā* | *yaṁ lavdha......ta....āsīt* | *sahasra....sramavirāhana caturdasyām-ārambha-rāma iti yaḥ sphuṭatām=upetaḥ* || *Asyāṁ bhū................*

(13) *-pā dharmmeṇa maryādayā rājya-Śrībhir-alaṁkṛtāḥ punar-amī bhog-aikadā.. ......Śrī-viśvāvidhe* (?) *eṣa kīrttana-kathā gīya..........*

(14) r *Kīrtti....tvām vismayakara.......āpi sauryyād=asau....nta*|*Śrīr-api...... ni...ddhi punar-īdriśī bhavati kiṁ Śrī Viśvarūp=oddhṛta-rekh-eva prati-pa........*

(15) *yat-te..ādbhutā | asy-aiva....Prapitāmahasya mahatīm-asthāpya kīrttim... ....tataḥ sādhitaḥ | Uddhṛtārthi-nisargga-dharmma-nirato yo...........*

(16) *.......siddhim-anayat-tām-eva kīrttim punaḥ || Kiṁ vrumaḥ........yasy-āsādhu-guṇasya nāsti mahataḥ ....kinna......*

(17) *rāśiḥ suviśṛtavayo yen-ākasmika-vismayena mukhar-ālokaḥ karttur-agri...... ....nivasanaḥ sphurad-dhārāgāraṁ visṛja.........*

(18) *-vyāmvara-saṁcara-tṛptir-vvahu-manoja.... ... | praśamanaṁ surā-bhāṇḍaṁ jaladaḥ || .....kanakeśvara......jaladaḥ....Śrī Viśvarūp-āvaro........*

(19) *tya sadācarau suviditaḥ Śrī-satkulā....sarvvaśaḥ satkulādṛto' kṣayavaṭo devo Vaṭeś-āhvayaḥ || Ity-ādyāḥ sumanonurūpa-racanā-ratnā................*

(20) *-jñāṁ ca yaḥ | Yen-āty-adbhuta-vikramena tarasā Śrī-mad-Gaya-maṇḍale āsaṁsāram-udagra-dharmma-vijaya-stambhā iv-āropitaḥ || Ten-ā i........*

(21) *-la visamaṁ nīhār-āvatārādbhutaṁ || Kirttiḥ Śveta-gabhasti-hasta-racite iti-rāja-tāṁ devasya Prapitā-mahasya mahatī Śrī-i...........*

(22) *-ti nāmadheya | Sattvaiva dhaninaḥ kimvā vahu vrumahe | kiṁ tv=īdṛg=yadi kirttanaṁ bhagavataḥ ken=āpi niṣpādita Śrī-Viśvāvi..................*

(23) *yaḥ svatvapa-mokṣa (?) | —yāvac-candra-divākarau surasarid-dhātrī nabho-maṇḍalaṁ | karttuṁ Kīrttikadamba (?) s a vijayī-Śri-Viśvarūp-āhvaye....*

(24) *gaṇitum-ālaṁkārito bhagavān bharttur-Vigraha-pāladeva-nṛpate rājyaśrīyaṁ vibhrataḥ | saṁprāpte tarasaiva pañch-gaṇite rajyasya samvatsa re..........*

(25) *Viśvāditya-guṇ-otkṣepa prītis-timita-cetasā*

(26) *Praśastir-vvihitā c=aiṣā Vaidya-Śrī-Dharmmapāṇinā ||.*

The original stone has suffered very much from the effects of weather so that it is almost impossible to decipher the central portions of the lines at the middle of the inscription. The only other known inscription of this king is the Bihar inscription of the twelfth year noticed for the first time by Cunningham.[1] He states that it is inscribed in the pedestal of an image of Buddha and belonged to the Broadley collection. The contents of the Broadley collection, afterwards called the Bihar Museum, were added to those of the Indian Museum at the request of the Government of Bengal in 1895 and the collection was transferred to Calcutta under the supervision of the late Babu Pūrṇa Chandra Mukharji. But this inscription could not be traced in the Indian Museum either by the late Dr. Bloch or by his successors. Mention should be made in this connection of an inscription on a stone on which the present image of Gadādhara at Gayā now rests. It seems to have been discovered by the late Babu Pūrṇa Chandra Mukharji and pointed out by him to the late Dr. Bloch.[2] As the image of Gadādhara cannot be moved without wounding the religious susceptibilities of the Hindu population of Gaya, only the first five lines could be copied :—

(1) *Oṁ namo mārttaṇḍāya || Jāgartti yasmin-nudite prayāti c-āstantu śete*

[1] Ind. Ant., Vol. XIV, p. 121, No. 7.

[2] Annual Report of the Archl. Survey, E. Circle., 1901-2, p. 2.

janatā samastā । *Trailokya dīpam tam-ananta-mūrttim-avyāhatābhaṁ.*
śaraṇaṁ prayāta ॥ (1).

(2) *S-eyaṁ vrahmapuri Gay-eti jagati khyātā svayaṁ vedhasā sthātuṁ vrahma-vidāṁ pur-īva ghaṭitā mokṣasya saukhyasya ca* |

(3) *Vrumaḥ kiñ-ca bhavanti yatra pitaraḥ pretālaya-vāsinaḥ pāda-spṛṣṭa-jala-pradāna-vidhinā nāk-āṅganā-nāyakāḥ* ॥ (2). *Asyāṁ va-*

(4) *-bhūva purī vakragati dvijihva samrāḍ-bhujaṅga ripur-acyuta-pādasevī* |
Yo nāma viṣṇu-rathavad-dvijarāja-varyaḥ prītyā satāṁ ca Pa

(5) *-ritoṣa iti prasiddhah* ॥ *Tasmād-vidheriva vabhūva........*

This inscription has been referred to the reign of Vigrahapāladeva because its writing resembles that of the Akṣayavaṭa inscription.

Nothing is known about the relations of Vigrahapāla III save his three sons Śūrapāla II, Mahīpāla II and Rāmapāla, all of whom succeeded him one after another.

Successors and relations.

The Rāmacarita mentions two uncles of Rāmapāla, Mahaṇa or Mathanadeva and his brother Suvarṇadeva, who belonged to the Rāṣṭrakūṭa family. So Vigrahapāla must have married another lady of the Raṣṭrakuṭa family whose name has not come down to us. Rāmapāla was the son of the Raṣṭrakuṭa princess and not of the Cedi princess Yauvanaśrī.

CHAPTER V.

The Decline of the Pālas.

After the death of Vigrahapāla III, his eldest son Mahīpāla II ascended the throne of his ancestors. According to the author of Rāmacarita, untoward things began to happen in this reign.[1] He did not act according to the advice of his ministers and was not well disposed towards his remaining brothers Śūrapāla and Rāmapāla. He was told by the people that Rāmapāla was an able Prince, as well as a popular and vigorous administrator, and that he would kill him and take away his kingdom. So, by low cunning, he tried to kill him, and at last succeeded in confining him in a prison.[2] It appears that Mahīpāla's younger brother Śūrapāla was sent to prison at the same time as his youngest brother Rāmapāla:—*Apareṇa bhrāttrā Śūrapālena saha kaṣṭāgāraṁ kārāgṛhaṁ mahattavanam rakṣaṇam yatra.*[3] This Śūrapāla was older than Rāmapāla, because the author of the Rāmacarita states, that Rāmapāla's son succeeded to the throne, though Śūrapāla was Rāmapāla's elder.[4] The brothers were reduced to very great straits while in prison.[5] The author adds in another place that both brothers were sent to prison because Mahīpāla had apprehensions of being dethroned by them.[6] About this time Divvoka, a former servant, by cunning, took away a part of Rāmapāla's paternal kingdom Varendrī.[7] Mahīpāla went to fight against the confederate rebels with the small force at his command and fell in battle. This happened while Rāmapāla was in prison.?[8] Elsewhere it is specified that the Kaivartta King killed Mahīpāla.[9] After Mahīpāla's death Rāmapāla seems to have been set free, but driven out of the country, as the author of Rāmacarita states, that Rāmapāla became careless of his body and mind, because he was kept out of his kingdom.[10] Nothing is known about the period following the death of Mahīpāla II up to the accession of Rāmapāla. Śūrapāla II seems to have been recognized by the adherents of the Pāla Princes as the successor of Mahīpāla II, as he is mentioned by name in the Manahali grant of Madanapāladeva. The importance of this grant lies in the fact that it does not ignore a single king of the Pāla dynasty from Gopāla I to Madanapāla. Thus it might have omitted the names of Gopāla III and Kumārapāla, because these two Princes are not ascendants of Madanapāla and such names are usually omitted in the genealogical part of a copperplate grant. If Śūrapāla II had not actually reigned his name would have surely been omitted from this grant. For a

Accession of Mahīpāla II, imprisonment of the Princes Rāmapāla and Śūrapāla. Rebellion in Northern Bengal.

War in Northern Bengal. Death of Mahīpāla II.

Accession of Śūrapala II, ignored by Sandhyākara Nandi but recorded in the Manahali grant of Madanapāla.

1 Comm. on V 31, p. 29, Mem. A.S.B., Vol. III.
2 Comm. on V 37, SC. L.C., p. 31.
3 Comm. on V 33, L.C.. p. 29.
4 Comm. on V 28, L.C., p. 28.
5 Comm on V 35, L.C., p. 28.
6 Comm. on V 36, L.C., p. 36.
7 Comm. on V 38, L.C., p. 31.
8 Comm. on V 31, L.C., p. 29.
9 Comm. on V 29, L.C., p. 28.
10 Comm. on V 41, L.C., p. 32.

similar reason we do not find the name of Rājyapāla, the eldest son of Rāmapāla, who could not have reigned as he died in his father's lifetime:—

Vigrahapāla III
- Mahīpāla II
- Śūrapāla
- Rāmapāla
  - Rājyapāla (died in his father's lifetime)
  - Kumārapāla
    - Gopāla III.
  - Madanapāla.

The mention of Śūrapāla's accession to the throne or the recognition of his chiefship in the Pāla dominions, may have been omitted by Sandhyākaranandi, either through carelessness, or as not being relevant to his subject. It may also be possible that Śūrapāla was Rāmapāla's rival for the throne, and though he had succeeded temporarily he was overthrown in the long run and perhaps murdered at the instigation of his younger brother. Nothing is known about the extent of Śūrapāla's reign or his death. But it is quite certain that he was succeeded by his younger brother Rāmapāla. In the course of time Divvoka had died and was succeeded by his brother Rudoka. Rudoka was succeeded by his son Bhīma, who on his succession, began to harass the people, living in the tract of land, which was still left in the possession of the Pālas.[1] At that time Rāmapāla was in great straits and thought himself to be without friends.[2] But his son and his advisors sought him, and urged him to take the necessary steps, and he regained courage.[3] The author of the Rāmacarita states in another place that he became very anxious to fight with Bhīma.[4] His first step was to travel round the country to propitiate the feudatories and subordinate kings of his father's kingdom, and he succeeded in gaining over the forest feudatories.[5] During his travels he became convinced that all feudatories were well disposed towards him.[6] By giving away lands along river banks and immense wealth, Rāmapāla succeeded in obtaining horse and foot soldiers and elephants from the feudatories. Śivarāja, the son of his maternal uncle and a Mahāpratīhāra, crossed the Ganges with foot, horse and elephants and entered the enemy's country.[7] This expedition was undertaken either to reconnoitre the enemy's position or as a sort of counter raid. Śivarāja so impetuously attacked Varendrī that the viṣayas and grāmas in Bhīma's country became distressed. Śivarāja began to enquire about the ownership of the lands so that the properties of the gods and the Brāhmaṇas might be protected.[8] He succeeded in driving away Bhīma's followers from Vārendrī proper[9], and then came back to

Rāmapāla is urged by his son and his friends to take the field against Bhīma.

He obtains aid from the feudatories and his cousin Śivarāja crosses the Ganges and enters the enemy's country.

[1] Comm. on V 39, L.C., p. 31.
[2] Comm. on V 40, L.C., p. 31.
[3] Comm. on V 26, L.C., p. 27.
[4] Comm. on V 43, L.C., p. 32.
[5] Comm. on V 43, L.C., p. 32.
[6] Comm. on V 44.
[7] Comm. on V 47, L.C., p. 33.
[8] Comm. on V 48, L.C., p. 34.
[9] Comm. on V 40, L.C.

report to Rāmapāla that his paternal kingdom was free of intruders.[1] Sandhyākara Nandi is silent about the events which followed this raid into Vārendrī. It appears from the second chapter of his work that the effect of Śivarāja's success in Northern Bengal was only temporary, because it became necessary for Rāmapāla to lead another and much bigger army into Northern Bengal, accompanied by his principal feudatories. One particular incident in the life of Rāmapāla has been totally left out by his biographer, which is his enmity and wars with Devarakṣita of Pīṭhī. In the commentary of the 8th verse of the second chapter of his work Sandhyākaranandi hints that Mahaṇa, the maternal uncle of Rāmapāla, recovered the kingdom, as the Boar incarnation had recovered the earth in former days. There is no reference to the enmity which Devarakṣita, the Lord of Pīthī and of Sindhu, bore towards Rāmapāla, which has become known to us from the Sārnāth inscription of Kumāradevi discovered by Messrs. Marshall and Konow in 1906-7.[2] It is stated there, that Mahaṇa, the King of Aṅga, the venerable maternal uncle of the Kings, conquered Devarakṣita in war, and maintained the glory of Rāmapāla, which rose in splendour, because the obstruction caused by his force was removed :—

Taṁ jitvā yudhi Devarakṣitam-adhāt Śri Rāmapālasya.
Yo lakṣmīṁ nirjita-vairi-rodhanatayā dedīpyamānodayāṁ.

verse 7.[3]

The defeat of Devarakṣita and Mahaṇa is also mentioned in the Rāmacarita, where it is said that Mathana or Mahaṇa defeated the King of Pīṭhī from the back of the elephant Vindhyamāṇikya.[4] The relationship between Mathanadeva and Rāmapāla has been explicitly mentioned in the commentary on verse 8, Chapter II of the Rāmacarita, so the references about Mathanadeva in the Sarnath inscription of Kumāradevī are quite clear. He is called the maternal uncle of the King because he was the maternal uncle of Rāmapāla, and perhaps also of Śūrapāla and Mahīpāla II also. Besides these, the sons of his other sisters might have been reigning in other parts of the country also. The mention of the defeat of Devarakṣita by Mathana or Mahaṇa is significant. The Sarnath inscription of Kumāradevī leaves no doubt about the fact that Mathana relieved Rāmapāla by defeating Devarakṣita. Evidently Devarakṣita of Pīthī had taken the part of one of Rāmapāla's rival claimants to the throne or invaded the Pāla dominions at a time when the Pāla kings were weakened by the defection of Northern Bengal, and so he expected to have an easy victory. The materials at our disposal are quite insufficient for the narration of details, but the Sarnath inscription of Kumāradevī proves, that though Mathana had humbled Devarakṣita at first, he had subsequently, owing to some unknown reason, given his daughter Śaṅkaradevī in marriage to him.[5] The probable reason is that either Devarakṣita succeeded in defeating Mathana and a peace was concluded after the marriage, or that Śaṅkaradevī was given to Devarakṣita in order to draw him to the party of Mathana and Rāmapāla. Whatever may be the fact of the case, we are sure that

Devarakṣita of Pīṭhī and Mathanadeva of Magadha.

[1] Comm. on V 50, L.C. [2] Annual Rep. of A.S. of India, 1907–8, p. 76. [3] Ep. Ind., Vol. IX, 324–26. [4] Mem. A.S.B., Vol. III, p. 38, Comm. on V 8. [5] Epi. Ind. Vol. IX, p. 322.

Devarakṣita did not continue to be the ruler of Pīthī for a long time, as we find another king in that country when Rāmapāla led his expedition into Northern Bengal. The relationship between the Pālas, the Gāhaḍavālas, the Rāṣṭrakūṭas of Magadha and the rulers of Piṭhī are shown in the table on following page.

Piṭhī has been identified by Dr. Sten Konow with the modern Piṭhapuram in the Madras Presidency.[1] But this is perhaps wide of the mark. It is mentioned as a separate principality, the ruler of which makes war upon the Pāla Kings of Bengal, and later on during the war between the Pālas and the Kaivartta King of Bengal, another prince of Piṭhī is mentioned as a feudatory or as an ally of the Pāla King.

The Position of Piṭhī.

It was hardly possible for the Pāla Kings after Nayapāla and Vigrahapāla III to wage war with the princes of Piṭhapuram or to demand an acknowledgment of suzeraint from them for any length of time. On the other hand, Piṭhi should be somewhere near Magadha or a province with a boundary contiguous to the possession of the Pālas. A place named Pīṭhaghaṭṭā is mentioned in an ancient geographical work called Deśāvalī,[2] a copy of which is in the manuscript collection of the Asiatic Society of Bengal. The addition of the word *ghaṭṭā* probably means that his place was situated on the Ganges. This Piṭha or Piṭhī was most probably on the western or northern boundary of Magadha and is perhaps represented by the trans-Son districts or Tirhut in the modern days. Some coins bearing the name Paṭha (most probably Piṭhī) are preserved in the Cabinet of the Indian Museum,[3] but no records are available to prove their find-spots.

Campaign in Varendrī.

The great event of Rāmapāla's reign was his campaign in Northern Bengal, against the descendants of the rebel Divvoka, in which he was assisted and accompanied by a large number of allies and feudatories. A long list of these princes is given, at the beginning of the second Chapter of Sandhyākaranandi's Rāmacarita

Allies and feudatories.

Unfortunately very few of the localities mentioned in this list can be identified at present. At the head of the list is the name of Bhīmayaśas, Prince of Piṭhī and Magadha. This prince is apparently

Bhīmaysas of Piṭhī and Magadha

the sucessor of Devarakṣita, as in one of the following verses the commentary describes the defeat of Devarakṣita by Mahaṇa as an already accomplished fact.[4] It may be that Devarakṣita had placed his son Bhīmayaśas on the throne after his defeat by Mahaṇa. The commentary distinctly states, that Bhimayaśas was Lord of Pīthi and Magadha,[5] but in the commentary on the Rāmacarita Mahaṇa is called Lord of Magadha, and Devarakṣita, King of Sindhu and Piṭhī. Mahaṇa may have been divested of the possession of Magadha by Bhimayaśas of Piṭhī, after his defeat of Devarakṣita and the marriage of Mahaṇa's daughter with him. It also appears that though Devarakṣita was the Lord of Piṭhī and Sindhu, his successor Bhīmayaśas was not. The position of Sindhu is doubtful. Bhīmayaśas is said to have

---

1 Ibid. 2 J.A.S.B. 1904, Pt. I, p. 178, note 1. 3 V. A. Smith Cat. of Coins, Ind. Mus, Vol. I, p. 263.
4 Mem. A.S.B., Vol. III, p. 38, Comm. on V. 9. 5 L.C. p. 36, Comm. on V. 5.

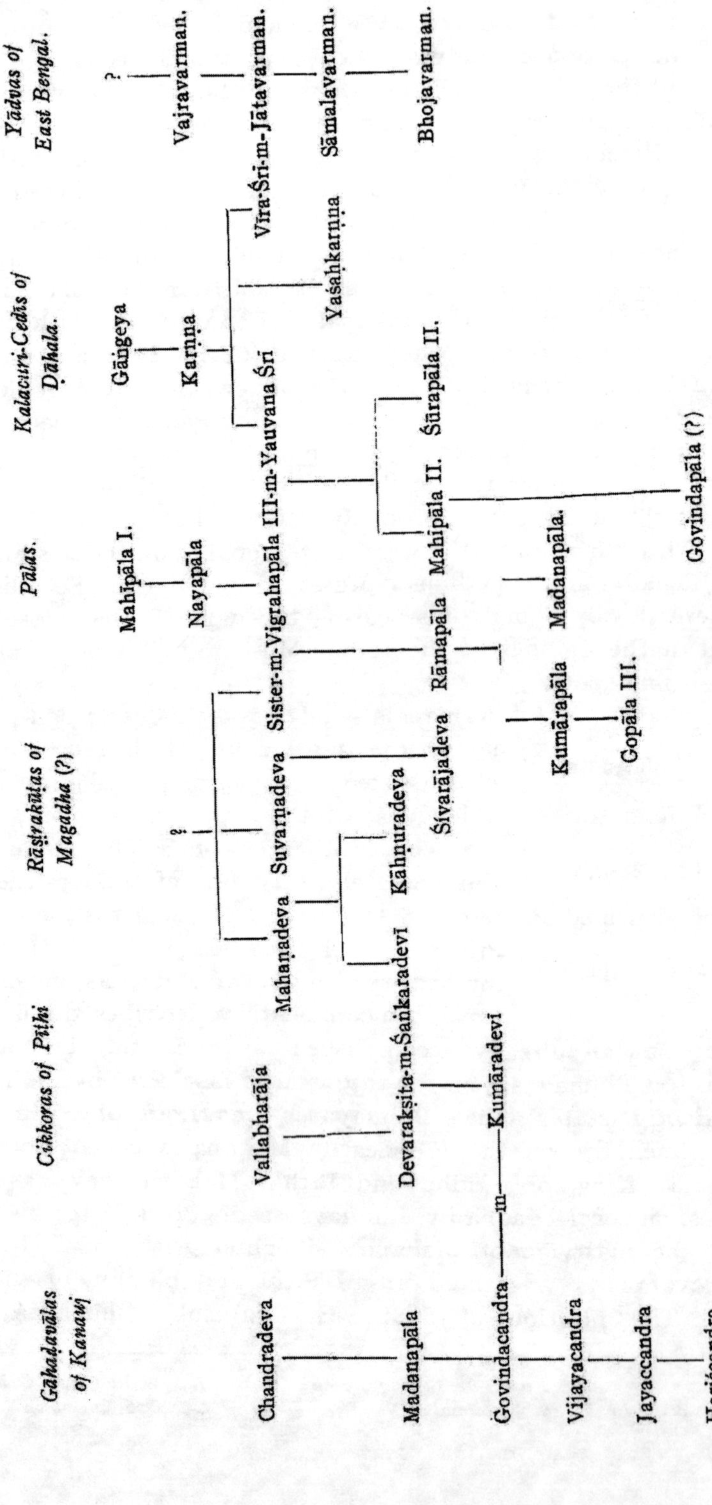
Gāhaḍavālas of Kanauj
Chandradeva
Madanapāla
Govindacandra —m— Kumāradevī
Vijayacandra
Jayaccandra
Hariścandra
Cikkoras of Pīṭhi
Vallabharāja
Devarakṣita-m-Śaṅkaradevī
Rāṣṭrakūṭas of Magadha (?)
?
Mahaṇadeva
Suvarṇadeva
Sister-m-Vigrahapāla III-m-Yauvana Śrī
Kāhṇuradeva
Śivarājadeva
Pālas.
Mahīpāla I.
Nayapāla
Rāmapāla
Mahīpāla II.
Śūrapāla II.
Kumārapāla
Madanapāla.
Gopāla III.
Govindapāla (?)
Kalacuri-Cedis of Ḍāhala.
Gāṅgeya
Karṇṇa
Yaśaḥkarṇṇa
Yādvas of East Bengal.
Vajravarman.
Vīra-Śrī-m-Jātavarman.
Sāmalavarman.
Bhojavarman.

defeated the troops of a king of Kānyakubja, whose name has not been discovered as yet. The position of Pīṭhī is also indicated by this reference. It seems to have been a buffer state between those of Kānyakubja and Gauḍa. The Pratīhāra dynasty was falling, and the kingdom of the proud Gāhaḍavāla was rising on its ruins. It is quite possible that Bhimayaśas of Pīṭhī assisted Candradeva, the Gāhaḍavāla, to obtain the city of Kānyakubja and to overthrow the last Gurjara-Pratīhāra King. The next prince in the order adopted by Sandhyākaranandi is Vīraguṇa of the forest of Koṭā, who is also styled "the over-lord of the Southern thrones." But nothing is known about this king. Dr. Kielhorn's lists of Northern and South Indian Inscriptions do not contain any record which mentions this king of the South. Jaya Simha, the Lord of Daṇḍabhukti, seems to have been a man of great importance. The position of Daṇḍabhūkti has already been indicated.[1] It is represented at the present day by the District of Midnapur. So Jaya Simha was the march-lord of the South. The commentary very appropriately mentions the defeat of the King Karṇakeśarī of Utkala by this prince. It is more natural for the King of Orissa to fight with a prince, whose land lay on his border, than with one, whose possessions were separated from his by a belt of mountains and forests. The position of Devagrāma in Vāla-valabhī, the king of which, Vikrama Keśarī, comes next in order, is far less certain. The commentary adds: "Devagrāma-prativaddha-vasudhā-cakravāla-vālavalabhī-taraṅga-vahala-galahasta-praśasta hastavikramo."[2] The explanation of this is not quite certain and nothing can be made out beyond what has already been stated by Mahāmahopādhyāya Hara Prasāda Sāstri. Vikrama Keśarī was the King of Devagrāma and the surrounding country which was washed by the rivers of Vāla-valabhi. Vāla-valabhī has been identified by Pandit Hara Prasāḍa Sāstrī with Bāgaḍī, one of the five divisions into which Bengal proper was divided before the Muhammadan conquest, but no reliable authority whatsoever can be cited in support of it. The name Vāla-valabhī itself was unknown in Bengal before the discovery of the Bhuvaneśvara prasasti of Bhavadevabhaṭṭa[3] and has not been found anywhere else except the Rāmacarita. There are hundreds of villages in Bengal bearing the name of Devagrāma, and I do not find any reason to confine it to one of them. Even in the Nadiāh district itself there are several Devagrāmas, and so the attempt to identify it with the materials at present at our command is premature. Lakṣmīśūra is said to be the Madhusūdana of another Mandāra and is described as the head of all Forest feudatories "*Samast-āṭavika-sāmanta-cakracuḍāmaṇiḥ.*"[4] The Mandāra mentioned here seems to be the hill of that name at present in the Bhagalpur district of Bihar. Mandāra hill commands the surrounding hilly and forest country to a great distance, and it may be that its king

Vīraguṇa of the South.

Jaya Simha of Daṇḍabhūkti.

Vikrama-Keśari of Devagrāma in Vāla-valabhī.

The position of Vālavalabhi.

Lakṣmīśūra of Maṇdāra.

[1] See Ante, p 71.

[2] Comm. on V. 5, Chap. II, p. 36.

[3] Ep. Ind. Vol. VI, p. 205.

[4] Comm. on V. 5, Ch. II, p. 36.

lorded over the Saontals of the Forest. The name of the next prince is suggestive.

Śūrapāla of Kujabaṭī.

Śūrapāla is mentioned as being the chief of Kujabaṭī. The Tirumalai inscriptions mention a feudatory of Mahīpāla I, named Dharmmapāla, who ruled over Daṇḍabhūkti.[1] Perhaps these princes belonged to the minor branches of the Imperial Pāla Dynasty. Rudraśikhara of Tailakampa is mentioned as a great warrior. Perhaps Mahāmahopādhyāya Hara Prasāda Śāstrī's identification[2] of Tailakampa with the modern Telkupi[3] in the Manbhum district is correct, but there is no proof in support of it beyond the resemblance in place names.

Rudraśikhara of Tailakampa.

Mayagala-siṁha of Ucchāla was the king of a country which was partly surrounded by the sea. The commentary mentions "*Aparalohitārṇava*" which means another Red Sea, but it is quite possible that the poet intends to mention the river Brahmaputra which is also known as the *Lauhitya*.

Mayagala-siṁha of Ucchāla.

Pratāpa-siṁha of Ḍekkarīya is also extolled in the commentary as a great warrior. There is nothing in the commentary to indicate the position of Ḍekkarīya, but it has been identified by Mahāmahopādhyāya Hara Prasāda Śāstri with the modern village of Ḍhekura or Ḍhekurī in the northern part of the Burdwan District, on the ground of similarity of names.[4] The commentary on the next verse mentions five princes, and among the names of places over which they ruled only two can be identified:—

Pratāpa-siṁha of Ḍekkarīya.

(1) Narasiṁhārjjuna, the king of the Kayaṅgala *maṇḍala*;
(2) Candārjjuna of Śaṅkaṭagrāma;
(3) Vijayarāja of Nidrāvala;
(4) Dorapavarddhana of Kauśāmbī; and
(5) Soma of Paduvanvā.

Dorapavarddhana of Kauśāmbi seems to have been a landlord of Varendrī. Kauṣāmbī seems to be the ancient name of the modern Pargana of Kusumba in the Rajshahi District of Bengal. I am indebted to Prof. Jadunath Sarkar of the Patna College for this suggestion. Paduvanvā has been identified by Mahāmahopādhyāya Hara Prasāda Sāstrī with the modern Pabna on the ground of similarity of names.

At the bottom of the list of feudatories we find mention of Rāmapāla's cousins on his mother's side, viz. the princes of the Rāṣṭrakūṭa family, and his eldest son Rājyapāla, who died in his life-time. Rāmapāla's maternal relations are specified in the next verse, his eldest maternal uncle Mathanadeva, whom we have already met, his brother Suvarṇadeva and their sons, the Mahāmāṇḍalika Kāhṇuradeva, and the Mahāpratīhāra Śivarājadeva.[5]

Rāmapāla's son and cousins.

Rāmapāla, with his allies and feudatories, crossed the Ganges either on boats or by a bridge of boats. The commentary on the next verse states that the great army

1 Epi. Ind., Vol. IX, p 232.

2 Mem. A.S.B., Vol. III, p. 14.

3 Cunningham's Arch. Surv. Report, Vol. VIII, p. 169.

4 Mem. A.S.B., Vol. III, p. 14.

5 Comm. on V. 8, Mem. A.S.B., Vol. III, p. 38.

crossed the Ganges by a 'Naukā-melaka'[1], which has been interpreted by Mahāmahopādhyāya Hara Prasāda Śāstri as "a bridge of boats." The commentary on the work does not specify the place where the battle took place, but it is quite certain that the contending armies met somewhere in the south-western part of the modern District of Rājshāhī, or the southern part of the Maldah District. According to the commentary on verse 16, Bhīma was captured alive during the battle, and the soldiers of Rāmapāla received a fresh impetus from the news.[2] The commentary on another verse states that Bhīma was captured on the back of an elephant.[3] Bhīma's army most probably dispersed on the capture of their leader, and Rāmapāla seems to have obtained an easy victory, which was followed by the sack of the town of Ḍamara, the capital of Bhīma.[4] The commentary on another verse states that Rāmapāla destroyed Ḍamara, a small town. The adjective *Upapura* is no doubt applied slightingly because it happened to be the capital of the enemy. Bhīma remained a captive and was placed in charge of a certain Vittapāla.[5] The scattered forces of Bhīma were rallied by one of his friends named Hari. In the ensuing battle Rāmapāla's son contested every inch of ground and at last succeeded in defeating the *Kaivarttas*. Hari was, at last, deprived of his forces, captured and executed with Bhīma. Ḍamara seems to have continued its existence after its sack by Rāmapāla, and even to this day a village named Ḍamaranagara exists close to Rāmapāla's capital. In another verse, Rāmapāla is said to have taken into employ the soldiers of Bhīma.[6] Rāmapāla founded a city named Rāmāvatī at the confluence of the Karatoyā and the Ganges.[7] The site seems to have been selected for Rāmapāla by a chief named Caṇḍeśvara of Śrī-hetu (not Śrī-haṭṭa) and one Kṣemeśvara.[8] The city was beautified within a very short time, and the author has devoted the best part of a chapter to its praise. The only feature, worth mentioning, is a Buddhist Vihāra named Jagaddala-Mahāvihāra, which was built by Rāmapāla in the new city. It is interesting to note that there is a village named Jagaddala close to the ruins of Rāmāvatī. Rāmāvatī continued to be the capital of the Pālas for some time, and Madanapāla's Manahali grant was issued from this place.[9] It continued to be a place of importance for several centuries. In the sixteenth century it gave its name to a fiscal division, and one of the circles in the Sirkar of Lakhnauti was named Ramauti[10] in Akbar's time. Ramauti is an exact transliteration of *Rāmāvatī* as Lakhnauti is of *Lakṣmaṇāvatī*, and the identity of Ramauti with Rāmāvatī has been made certain by the discoveries of Babu Haridās Pālit in the Maldah District. This gentleman has industriously searched the environments of Rāmāvatī and has traced

The campaign, a bridge of boats on the Ganges.

The battle. Capture of Bhīma on the back of an elephant.

The sack of Ḍamara, the enemy's capital.

Rebellion of Hari, defeat, capture and execution with Bhīma.

Foundation of a capital—Rāmāvatī.

---

[1] L. C. Comm. on V. 10, p. 38.
[2] Comm. on V. 16, L.C., p. 40.
[3] Comm on V. 20, L.C., p. 41.
[4] Comm. on V. 27, Chap. I, L.C., p. 27.
[5] L.C., p. 14; V. 36, Ch. II, p. 45.
[6] V. 38. Mem. A.S B., Vol. III. p. 46
[7] V. 10, Ch. III, L.C., p. 47.
[8] V. 2, Ch. III, L.C.
[9] J.A S.B., 1900, pt. I.
[10] J.R.A.S., 1894, Ain-i-Akbari, Bib. Ind., Vol. II, p. 131.

the following villages bearing ancient names: *Amrauti* or *Ramrauti* (*Rāmāvatī*), Jagadalā (*Jagaddala*), Ḍāmrol (*Ḍamara*).

After the foundation of Rāmāvatī, Rāmapāla engaged in wars with his neighbours. He attacked Utkala and ruled the country up to Kaliṅga,[1] and returned the kingdom of Utkala to the Nāgavaṁśa. His feudatory chief Māyana conquered Kāmarūpa which seems to have been becoming weaker and weaker at this time, as several invasions into that country were led by successive kings of Bengal or their generals, e.g., Māyana sent by Rāmapāla, Vaidyadeva sent by Kumārapāla, Vijayasena and Lakṣmaṇasena. A king of Eastern Bengal sought the protection of Rāmapāla in order to save himself by surrendering to him his best elephants, his coach of state and his armour.[2]

Later wars of Rāmapāla.

Svaparitrāṇanimittaṁ patyā yaḥ prāg-diśīyena :.
Vara-vāraṇena ca nija-syandana-dānena varmmaṇārādhe ||.

Rāmacarita III. 44.

This king seems to be one of the Yādavas of Eastern Bengal. Two different powers may have caused him to throw himself under the protection of Rāmapāla: first is an invasion by Pāla forces, and second an invasion of his territories by a new power. Sāmantasena was most probably getting very powerful at this time, and it was he who seems to have caused the Yādava prince to seek the shelter afforded by Rāmapāla.

In his later years Rāmapāla returned to Rāmāvatī, leaving the cares of the management of the state to his eldest son Rājyapāla.[3] About this time Mathanadeva, the king's maternal uncle, died. The king was residing at Mudgiri (*Mudgagiri* or *Mungir*) at this time,[4] and on hearing of his benefactor's death distributed much wealth to the Brāhmaṇas and entered the sacred river Ganges. Mathanadeva must have become a centenarian at the time of his death, and Rāmapāla himself had become a very old man at the time of his death after forty-six years of reign.

Death of Mathanadeva and Rāmapāla.

Tārānātha states that Rāmapāla reigned for forty-six years.[5] This is not impossible as the Caṇḍimau image was dedicated in the 42nd year of the king. We know the names of three of the sons of Rāmapāla, two of whom succeeded him on the throne. His eldest son, Rājyapāla, was an able man, and assisted his father in gaining the throne, in the wars in Vārendrī, and finally in administering the kingdom in his father's old age. He seems to have died during the lifetime of his father, as we find that Kumārapāla succeeded after Rāmapāla's death. His third son, Madanapāla, ascended the throne after the death or dethronement of his brother Kumārapāla's son Gopāla III. We know nothing about the other relations of Rāmapāla except his

Length of reign. Successors.

1 Mem. A.S B., Vol. III, p. 50, Ch. III, V. 45.

2 Mem. A.S.B., Vol III, p. 50. This has also been translated differently by Mr. Maitra. "A King of Eastern Bengal, who held the title of Varman, sought the protection of Ramapala in order to save himself by surrendering his elephants and chariot."

3 L.C., p. 51, Ch. IV, V. 6.

4 L.C., V. 9.

5 Ind. Ant., Vol. XXXVIII, p. 246.

maternal uncles, Mathanadeva or Mahaṇadeva and Suvarṇadeva and their sons Kāhṇuradeva and Śivarājadeva. Sandhyākaranandi's father, Prajāpatinandi, was the principal minister of peace[1] and war (*Mahāsāndhivigrahika*), but his principal adviser was Bodhideva, son of Yogadeva, the minister of his father Vigrahapāla III.[2]

Ministers.

The earliest record of Rāmapāla is the Tetrawan inscription recording the erection of an image of Tārā by a certain Bhaṭṭa Īcchara, in the 2nd year of the King's reign. This image was discovered by the late Mr. A. M. Broadley, who read the king's name as Rāmapati.[3] Cunningham published it in one of his reports.[4] The inscription was finally published by Babu Nilmani Chackravartti with a good ink impression in 1908.[5] It consists of two lines partly damaged, and is at present in the Indian Museum.

King's reign. Inscriptions and MS. Records.

The next record in order is a manuscript of the Aṣṭasāhasrikā Prajñāpāramitā written at Nālandā in the Magadha *viṣaya.* The manuscript was purchased by Dr. A. F R. Hoernle from Nepal, during his stay in India,[6] and afterwards acquired by the Bodleian Library.[7] It was written in the 15th year of the king and its final colophon runs as follows:—

1.—*ranuttara jñānāvāptaya iti, Mahārājādhirāja Parameśvara-Paramabhaṭṭāraka-Paramasaugata Śrimad = Rāmapāladeva-pravarddhamāna-vijayarājye pañcadaśame samvatsare abhilikhyamāne yatrāṁkenāpi samvat* 15, *Vaisākṣadıne kṛṣṇasaptamyām* 7 *Asti Magadhaviṣaye, Śrī Nālandāvasthita lekhaka Grahaṇakuṇḍena Bhaṭṭārikāpra-*

2.—*jñāpāramitā likhitā iti.*

Late in the king's reign an image of the Bodhisatva Padmapāṇi was dedicated, at or near the modern village of Chaṇḍimau in the Bihar Sub-division of the Patna District by an inhabitant of Rajagṛiha. This inscribed image was discovered by Cunningham in 1877 or 1878,[8] but he did not attempt to read it. No attempt has hitherto been made by anybody else to read this inscription. The image was found lying among the number of broken ones in the outskirt of the village of Chaṇḍimau in August 1911 and was removed to Indian Museum. A part of the inscription was broken owing to careless packing, but fortunately two inked impressions of the inscription were taken while *in situ*, otherwise it would have become quite impossible to read the date, as the part bearing the numerals for the year have disappeared. This is the most interesting part of the epigraph as it proves conclusively that Rāmapāladeva reigned for a considerable length of time, at least 42 years, which made Tāranātha's statement about his length of reign acceptable. Cunningham read the date as 12, but it certainly was 42. The inscription itself runs as follows :—

The date of the Chaṇḍimau Image.

(1). *Ye dharmmā hetu prabhavā hetu (ṁ) teṣām hy = avadat (t) eṣām (ṁ) yo nirod-*

---

1 L.C. p. 55, V. 3.
2 Epi. Ind., Vol. II, p. 348.
3 J.A.S.B. 1872, Pt. I, p. 282.
4 Cunningham's Arch. Survey Rep., Vol. III, p. 124.
5 J. and P.A.S.B., Vol. IV, p. 109, pl. vii.
6 J.A.S B., 1900, pt. I, p. 100.
7 Cat. Bodleian Liby., Cambridge, Vol. II, p. 250, No. 1428.
8 Cunningham Arch. Survey Rep., Vol. XI, p. 169.

dho evaṁ vādī mahāśramaṇaḥ । *Śrī-mad = Rājagṛha viniggatch Etrahāgrāmāvasthitaḥ* ‖ *Paramopāsaka paramamahājān (ānuv) āvinaḥ* ॥ *Vaṇika Sādhu.*

(2) *Saharaṇasya Sādhu Bhādulvasutasya yadatra puṇyaḥ* ‖ *Tad-bhavatv-ācaryopādhyāya-mātā-pita purvvaṅgama (ṁ) kṛtvā sakala (satva) rāser-ajñāna phalavāptaya iti* ॥ *Paramabhaṭṭāraka Parameśvara Paramasau (?)*

(3) .... *ta* । *Mahārajādhirāja Śrī-mad = Rāmapāladevapāda pravarddhamāna-kalyāṇa-vijayarājye samvat* 42 *Āṣāḍha dine* 30.

The date is given in the decimal notation so that there remains no doubt about its reading. The first numeral is certainly 4 and not 1. We find it in a contemporary inscription—the Bodh-Gaya inscription of the 74th year of the Lakṣmaṇasena era.[1] The donor, Sādhu Saharaṇa, was most probably Vaiṣya by caste and a merchant by profession. Nothing was known about Rāmapāla and his times twenty years ago. When Mr. Venis was editing the Kamauli grant of Vaidyadeva, he was faced with great difficulties for want of materials.[2] The date of Vaidyaveva's grant was fixed by him on conjecture. Recent discoveries have proved beyond doubt, that the grant must be placed half a century earlier. Rāmapāla's date was fixed and the events of his reign made known by the discovery of the Rāmacarita of Sandhyākaranandi [3] Nothing has been stated about, and the place of discovery of, this unique manuscript, by the discoverer himself, in the introduction to his edition of the Rāmacarita, but I have since its publication learnt on enquiry from him that the manuscript was purchased in Nepal in 1897 The manuscript itself consists of two different parts:—(1) The text, which is complete, and (2) the commentary, which is incomplete but older than the text. It runs up to the thirty-fifth verse of the second chapter of the text. The text of the work is written in Bengali characters of the 12th or 13th centuries on strips of palmleaf. It is,

The text of the Rāmacarita.

Mahāmahopādhyāya Hara Prasāda Śāstrī observes, written in imitation of the Rāghava-Pāṇḍavīya, in *double entendre.*[4] The difficulty of understanding such a work is apparent, and had it been discovered without its commentary, it would have been of no use to historians or antiquarians. The principal value of the discovery lies in the commentary. The commentary is a mine of historical information, and supplies the details of the events of Rāmapāla's reign. The style of the composition of the commen-

The Commentary.

tary is highly ornamental prose, which makes it very difficult for one to get at the truth. The text does not end after the death of Rāmapāla but continues to describe the events of the reigns of his successors, Kumārapala, Gopāla III, and Madanapāla. If the second part of the commentary is ever recovered, then an abundance of detail will be available, about the events of the time of the three princes mentioned above. There is very little doubt about the fact, that the author of the poem was obliged to

The Author.

write the commentary on it himself. The masses of details which are called up by the use of single works, would have

---

1 Ind. Ant., Vol. X, p. 346.

2 Epi. Ind., Vol. II, p. 348.

3 Proc. A.S.B., 1900, p. 70.

4 Mem. A.S.B., Vol. III, p. 1.

had no meaning to other persons. The author had great facilities for the collection of information as his father was Rāmapāla's Sāndhivigrahika. The comparison of Rāmapāla with Rāma, the hero of the Rāmāyaṇa, seems to have been habitual with the courtiers of the 11th century A.D. A verse of the Kamauli grant of Vaidyadeva mentions the conquest of Mithilā and a king named Bhīma, and at the same time compares Rāmapāla with Rama:—

Tena yena jagat=traye janaka-bhū-lābhād-yathāvad=yaśaḥ.
Kṣauṇī-nāyaka-Bhīma Rāvaṇa-vadhād-yuddhārṇṇav=ollaṁghanāt ||.

verse 4.[1]

According to Lama Tārānatha, Yakṣapāla was a colleague of Rāmapāla.[2] It is stated definitely that this prince was the son of Rāmāpāla who was the son of Hastipāla and was the last prince of the Pāla family.[3] An inscription of a king (*Narendra*) named Yakṣapāla was found at Gayā by Sir Alexander Cunningham and published by the late Dr. Kielhorn in 1887. But the king mentioned in this record cannot be the same person as that mentioned by Lama Tārānatha as Rāmapāla's son, as the genealogy of this Yakṣapāla is given in the inscription. He is the son of Viśvāditya, who built the temple of Gadādhara,[4] of Akṣayavaṭa and of Prapitāmaheśvara, the grandson of Śūdraka. The family was a very important one during the reigns of Nayapāla Vigrahapāla and his sons. The following inscriptions of the family have been discovered at Gaya:—

Yaksapala of Gaya.

(1) Inscription on the gate of the modern Kṛṣṇa-Dvārika temple, recording the erection of a temple of Viṣṇu by a low class Brāhmaṇa named Viśvāditya in the 15th year of Nayapāladeva.[5]

(2) Inscription inside the small temple dedicated to Narasiṁha in the courtyard of the Viṣṇupāda temple recording the erection of a temple to Gadādhara and several other minor shrines—by one Viśvarūpa of the same lineage as Viśvāditya in No. 1.[6]

(3) Inscription broken into two parts in the wall of small shrine under the Akṣayavaṭa at Gayā, recording the erection of two temples of Śiva—Vaṭeśa and Prapitāmahésvara—by the same Viśvāditya.[7]

(4) Inscription under the image of Gadādhara at Gayā—begins with an invocation to the Sun-god and mentioning Paritoṣa, the grandfather of Viśvāditya.[8]

(5) The Sītalā temple inscription of Yakṣapāla recording the erection of a temple dedicated to various deities and digging a tank named *Uttaramānasa*.[9]

The last inscription was published in 1887 and at that time the late Dr. Kielhorn was of opinion that "the characters of the inscription are Devanāgarī, or to be more particular, a kind of Devanāgarī, which appears to have been current in the 12th century A.D." But if the characters of this inscription are compared with those of the Narasiṁha temple inscription of Nayapāladeva, on the one hand, and the

---

1 Epi. Ind., Vol II. p. 351.
2 Ind. Ant., Vol. XXXVIII, p. 243.
3 Ibid., Vol. XVI, p. 64.
4 See ante, p. 79.
5 J.A.S.B. 1900, pt. I, pp. 192-93.
6 See ante, p. 78.
7 See ante, p. 81.
8 See ante, p. 82.
9 Ind. Ant., Vol. XVI, p. 64.

Gadādhara temple inscription of Govindapāladeva, it will be found that the characters of the inscription of Yakṣapala are more akin to those of Krisṇa-Dvārika, Narasiṁha temple and Akṣayavaṭa than to the latter. In my humble opinion the characters belong to the middle of the 11th century A.D. The inscription was edited without a facsimile and could not be traced easily. Kielhorn had stated that it had been found at Satighat in Gayā, but I could not find any Satighat or any old inscription. The inscription was eventually found hidden behind a door inside a small temple, on the side of a paved tank, called the Śītalā temple, close to the river Phalgu, and just behind the Gaya Zilla School. Dr. Kielhorn's edition is transcribed below, with the exception of the last word which he could not read from the rubbings :—

1. *Oṁ namaḥ Sūryāya || Viṣaya-madhūtkara-pūrṇṇaṁ Prāṇi-nikāy-āli viśva-śata patraṁ Aṣṭāśā-dala-ramyaṁ prakāśayan-navatu vo bhānuḥ ||.*

2. *Tīrthaṁ phalgu-taṭ-ādi-tīrtha-ghaṭanā-vyājena sopāninī gantṛṇāṁ paramasya dhauta-tamasāṁ dhāmno Gayā rājate । Śrī maty-aiva ya-*

3. *—yā mahīmaya-milac-citrasya jīv-ātmanā śilp-otkarṣam-amanyat-ātmani vidhiḥ kṛtvā trilokīm-api || Asyāṁ vabhūva ripu-vṛndam-a-*

4. *—nindya-sauryaḥ kurvvan-vana-praṇayi pattra-niketanasthaṁ । Śrī Śūdrakaḥ svayam-apujayad-indra-kalpo Gauḍeṣvaro nṛpati-lakṣaṇa-puja-*

5. *—yāyaṁ || Tasmād-adbuta-pauruṣāmvudhir-abhūt Śrī-Viśvarūpo nṛpaḥ kīrtti-śrī-matayaḥ svayaṁvaratayā bhejur-yam-ekaṁ patiṁ A*

6. *—dyāpi sphurad-ugra-vikrama-kathām-ākarṇṇayad-yasya ca svāsaṁbhūtim-arāti-cakram-asama-ttrāsāt-tadā ślāghate || Laksmīṁ ripoḥ*

7. *sva-bhuja-vīrya-vasīkṛtāṁ yo bhogyāṁ tathā vihitavān dvijapuṅgavānāṁ Eṣāṁ yathā yuvatayo dyutim-ādadhānā nā-*

8. *—kāṅganā iva virejur-ilātalepi || Yasy-ojvalena yaśasā bhramatā samantāccakre ciraṁ dhavalite vidiśāṁ di-*

9. *—Śāñ-ca lokeṣv-abhiprathayituṁ mṛga-lāñchanaḥ svaṁmeṇāṅkam-ulvaṇa mahar--nniśam-ādadhāti || Yen-ādy-āpi cakāśati prati-di-*

10. *—śaṁ devalayāḥ kāritā bhuyāṅso hima-dīdhiti-dyuti-muṣo mediny-alaṁkāriṇaḥ । Murtyāyāmatayā himādri-śikhara-spa-*

11. *—rddh-occhritair-mūrddhabhiḥ kurvvanto viyati skhaladgatiratham prasthā nadusthaṁ raviṁ || Dharmmasya hṛdya iva sūnur-ajātaśatrus-tasy-ātha-*

12. *dhairya-nilayo-jani Yakṣapālaḥ । Luptakratau Kaliyugasya vijṛmbhite yaḥ kāmān-bhṛśaṁ kratubhujaḥ kratubhiḥ pu—*

13. *—poṣa || Pluṣṭo-naṅgatayā pareṣv-ayam-ayaṁ bhikṣā-bhujā-nirjjitaḥ sarvveṇ āpy-avalā-valoyaṁ-acirasthāyī mano-bhūr-a-*

14. *yaṁ । Ity-anyo vidhinā manojña tanu-bhṛj-jetā dviṣāṁ yo bhujādaṇḍ-aika pravalaḥ sthiro yudhi sadā mīnadhvajo nirmmi-*

15. *—taḥ || Bhūbhāro rohana-bhūditara-taru-tulām-āśritaḥ kalpa-śākhī kiṁdhenuḥ kāmadhenuḥ kṣititala-parikhā kīrtti-*

16. *—pātraṁ payodhiḥ | Ity-āśann-ādi-dātṛin-prati jagati giro gīyamānā narendre yasminn-abhyarthamānair-vvasubhir-aviratam tarppayaty-arthisā-*

17. —*rthān* || *Yad-dhṛt-padma-kuṭīraka-praṇayitām-āpādite śrī-patau suprīte vyabhicāranītv-aratayā bhaktyā parikrīḍitam . Arthibhyo vi-*

18. —*niyuktay-āpy-anudinaṁ pātre sucau jātayā mat-svāmi-priyavāsa eṣa iti yaḥ kāmaṁ śriyā saṁśritaḥ* || *Maunāditya-Sahaśralinga-*

19. *Kamal-ārddhāṅgīṇa-Nārāyaṇa-Dvistomeśvara-Phalgunātha-Vijayādity-āhvayānāṁ kṛtī* ı *sa prāsādam-acīkarad-dviviṣadāṁ Kedāradevasya*

20. *ca khyātasy-Ottaramānasasya khananaṁ sattraṁ tathā c-ākṣaye* || *Sūrya-candramasau yāvad-yāvat kṣaunī sasāgara . Tāvat śrī Yakṣapālasya rā-*

21. —*jantāṁ bhuvi kīrttayaḥ* || *Nyāya-vidyā-vidāṁ śreyān-Āgīgrāma kulodbhavaḥ Śrī-Murārir-dvija-śreṣṭhaḥ praśastim-akarod-imām.*

22. *Likhit-āsau Śrī Padmapāṇinā* ||

The characters of this inscription cannot be said to belong to the 12th century A.D., as the form of the test letters are much earlier than those of RĀMAPĀLA. Most probably Yakṣapāla assumed independence during the troublesome times of the reigns of Vigrahapāla III, Mahīpāla II and Śūrapāla II. Perhaps he was contemporary of Rāmapāla during the earlier part of the latter's reign. He is not mentioned in the Rāmacarita, and most probably he was subdued by Rāmapāla's maternal uncle, Mathanadeva, who is styled *Magadhādhipa* in the commentary. He might have continued to reign either as a subordinate prince, or as an independent one, because no evidence is forthcoming to prove that any of the Pāla Emperors after Rāmapāla held any part of Western Magadha or South-Western Behar. Rāmapāla's inscriptions have been discovered in Eastern Magadha, but no Pāla record after the time of Vigrahapāla III have been found in the Gayā or Shahabad District, except the two inscriptions of Govindapāladeva. Another powerful dynasty of kings, who founded their monarchy on the ruins of the second Pāla Empire, was that of the Varmans of Eastern Bengal.

Four records of this dynasty have come to light as yet:—

(1) Bhuvaneśvara inscription of the time of Bhaṭṭa Bhavadeva.[1]

(2) The unpublished copper-plate grant of Harivarmmadeva, which has been noticed by Babu Nagendra Natha Basu in *Vaṅgera Jātīya Itihāsa*,'' Vol. II, p. 215 and plate. This copperplate grant was seen and examined by the author several years ago. It was obtained from the late Mr. Hari Nath De, and was photographed with the permission of the owner. Very little can be made out of the grant at present.

(3) A manuscript of the "*Aṣṭa-sāhasrikā Prajñāpāramitā*" written in the 19th year of Harivarmmadeva, recently acquired by me.

(4) The Belabo grant of Bhojavarman. According to the genealogy given in the inscription, the Varmans were descended from the race of Yadu In that race were a lines of princes, who ruled at Siṁhapura, which was in the Punjab, as we know from the Lakkha-mandal-praśasti of the Princess Īśvarā. Vajravarman of that dynasty was the founder of a kingdom in Eastern Bengal. His son, Jātavar-

[1] Epi. Ind., Vol. VI, p. 203.

man, was, as we have seen, the contemporary of Vigrahapāla III, who defeated the Cedī King Karṇṇa in Aṅga, and obtained the hand of his daughter Vira-Śrī, conquered Kāmarūpa and Govarddhana, and acquired paramount power. His son was Sāmalavarman, about whom we do not know much. The accounts of Sāmalavarman as found in the genealogical works are wholly imaginary. He was succeeded by his son Bhojavarman. The characters of the new grant show that Harivarman and his father Jyotirvarman cannot either be placed before Vajravarman or taken to be his descendants, because most probably Sāmantasena made an end of the Yādava kingdom of Eastern Bengal shortly afterwards. So it appears probable that the two dynasties were to some extent contemporaneous.

The first inscription has indeed been published by the late Dr. Kielhorn, but no facsimile was published at that time. A complete analysis of the characters of these three records or an attempt to fix the date of Harivarman would be out of place here. I intend very shortly to publish another paper on the inscription and the chronology of the Varman kings. It might suffice here to say that the copperplate of Harivarmmadeva, though in a very bad state of preservation, gives us the name of the king and his father. The last line of the first side and the first line of the second contained the following sentences:—

Mahārājādhirāja-Srīmad-Jyotirvarmmadeva-pādānudhyāta Paramavaiṣṇava-Parameśvara-Paramabhaṭṭāraka-Mahārājādhirāja Śrīmad-Harivarmmadeva kuśalī.

The grant itself was issued from the victorious camp of Vikramapura, and from it we learn that part at least of Eastern Bengal belonged to Harivarmmadeva and that he was preceded by his father Jyotirvarmmadeva on the throne. The characters of the records of those dynasties show that Harivarman cannot be placed in the 12th century A.D. Consequently it must be admitted that his father Jyotirvarmman has to be placed in the earlier decades of the 11th century. The dynasty seems to have continued for three or four generations. We learn from Bhuvaneśvara inscription that Bhavadeva I received the village of Hastinībhiṭṭa from the King of Gauḍa. His son was Rathāṅga, whose son was Atyaṅga, and from him was descended Ādideva, who was the minister of peace and war (*Sāndhivigrahika*) of the king of Vaṅga. It is stated in verse 3 that the family settled in the village of Siddhala in Rāḍhā. Ādideva's son was Govarddhana who was renowned as a warrior and most probably served under Jyotirvarmmadeva. His son Bhavadeva II was the minister of Harivarmmadeva and of his son also.

The newly discovered Belabo plate records the grant of 9 *droṇas* of land in the village of Upyalikā, in the sub-division of Kauśāmvi-Aṣṭagaccha in the *Maṇḍala* or District of Adhaḥpattana, in the Division or *Bhukti* of Pauṇḍravarddhana, to a Brāhmaṇa of the Yajur-deva, named Rāmadevaśarman, son of Viśvarūpadevaśarman, grandson of Jagannāthadevaśarman and great-grandson of Pitāmbaradevaśarman, who was an inhabitant of the village of Siddhala, in Northern Rāḍhā, and had emigrated from Madhyadeśa or Kanauj.

The last line of the Bhuvaneswar inscription of Bhavadeva contained his surname—

Vālavalabhī-bhujaṅga.

Vālavalabhī is mentioned as the name of a country in the Rāmacarita of Sandhyākaranandi. Vikramarāja of Devagrāma in Vālavalabhī had fought with Rāmapāla, in the war, in Varendra.[1] Mahāmahopādhyāya Haraprasād Sastri had identified Vālavalabhi with *Bāgḍī*. He translates the passage of the commentary as follows :—

" Vikramarāja, the Rājā of Devagrāma and the surrounding country, washed by the waves of the rivers of Vāla-Valabhī or Bāgḍi, one of the five provinces into which Bengal was divided." The identification stands without any support. From the description given in the commentary on the Ramacarita it appears that Vālavalabhī was pre-eminently a land of rivers, and must be identified either with Eastern or Southern Bengal. The mention of Vikramapura in the copperplate grant of Harivarman does not help us in fixing the chronology of the Varmans. It may be that both dynasties occupied different parts of East Bengal at the same time and may have laid claim to the ownership of the city of Vikramapur. So far we have no positive evidence to prove that Jyotirvarman and Harivarman were descended from the Yādava Vajravarman, and we can only assume that they belong to co-lateral branches of the same family.

The invasion of the great southern conqueror Rājendra Coḷa I seems to have left some permanent marks in Bengal. We learn from the Sītāhāṭī grant of Vallālasena, that the ancestors of Sāmantasena, the grandfather of Vijayasena, lived in the country of Rāḍhā.[2] All Sena inscriptions agree in stating that the Sena kings were descended from a family of Karṇāṭa Kṣatriyas, i.e. from a family which originally came from the Kanarese-speaking districts of Southern India. Though the Cālukya King, Vikramāditya VI of Kalyāna, is said to have invaded Bengal during the lifetime of his father Somesvara I,[3] it cannot be said that the Cālukya Kings effected any permanent conquest in Eastern India. But, on the other hand, Vīlhaṇadeva's remarks should be taken with great reservation, as none of the records of the Cedīs of Tripurī or Ratnapura mention any Cālukya invasion of Northern India in the middle of the 11th century A.D. On the other hand, Rājendra Coḷa I defeated the Cālukya King, Jayasiṁha II, at Muyaṅgi or Musaṅgi, and though Cālukyan poets state that the Cālukyas defeated the Coḷas, the definite terms of the Melpāḍi inscription leave no doubt about the fact that the defeat of the Cālukya Kings was decisive, and Rājendra Coḷa I obtained a large amount of treasure from him.[4] Some obscure Karṇāta Chief seems to have followed Rājendra Coḷa I and settled in Western Bengal after the defeat of his Chief on the banks of the Ganges. From him was descended Sāmantasena, who is generally taken to be the founder of the Sena Dynasty. He seems to have succeeded in carving out a small principality for himself in Western Bengal. In the Deopara *praśasti* of his grandson, Vijayasena, it is stated that he, Sāmantasena, defeated his enemies after being surrounded by them.[5]

---

1 Mem. A.S.B., Vol. III, p. 36, Comm. on V, p. 5.

2 Vangīya Sāhitya Pariṣad-Patrikā, Vol. XVII, Pt. IV, p. 235, v. 3.

3 *Vikramānkadeva Caritam.* (Ed. Bühler, III. 74).

4 South Indian Inscriptions, Vol. III, No. 18, p. 27.

5 Epi. Ind., Vol. II, p. 124.

None of the Sena Princes are mentioned in the list of Rāmapāla's feudatories, and most probably their relations with the Imperial Pālas were not cordial. Sāmanta-sena, probably, came to power during the disturbances, in the earlier part of the reign of Vigrahapāla III. We know nothing about his son, Hemantasena, who was most probably a very tame vassal of the Emperor Rāmapāladeva.

Officers.

Rāmapāla's minister was Bodhideva, the son of Yogadeva, who was the prime minister of his father Vigrahapāla III. His minister for peace and war (Sāndhi-vigrahika) was Prajāpatinandi, the father of Sandhyākaranandi. Māyana, one of his principal generals, conquered Assam[1] for him, and according to Mahāmahopādhyāya Haraprasād Śāstrī, his Chief Medical Officer was Bhadreśvara.[2]

[1] Mem A.S.B., Vol. III, p. 50, Comm. on v. 47.

[2] Ibid., p. 15.

CHAPTER VI.

THE LAST KINGS.

Rāmapāladeva was succeeded by his second son Kumārapāla about the year 1097 A.D. Immediately after Kumārapāla's accession, rebellions broke out throughout the kingdom. In Assam, which had been conquered for Rāmapāla by the feudatory chief Māyana, Tiṅgyadeva raised the standard of rebellion. Southern Bengal and Western Bengal were overrun by the King of Orissa, Anantavarmman *Coḍagaṅga*. Sandhyākaranandi dismisses Kumārapāla with a single verse:—

Kumārapāla.

> *Atha rakṣatā* (?) *Kumārodita pṛthu-paripanthi-pārthiva-pramadaḥ* । *Rājyam-upabhujya bharasya sūnur-agamad=divaṁ tanu-tyāgāt.* ||—v. 11.[1]

This most probably indicates that Kumārapāla reigned for a very short time. But during this short reign, he succeeded in obtaining decisive victories in Assam and in Southern Bengal with the aid of his Minister Vaidyadeva, who was the son of Yogadeva, the Prime Minister of Rāmapāla. We learn from the Kamauli Grant of Vaidyadeva that Kumārapāla having learnt of the disaffection of the feudatory chief of Kāmārūpa, named Tiṅgyadeva, deputed Vaidyadeva to overcome him. Vaidyadeva having received a promise of obtaining the kingdom after its conquest, reached Assam by forced marches and defeated Tiṅgyadeva:—

> *Etādṛśe hari-harid-bhuvi satkṛtasya Śrī-Tiṅgyadeva nṛpater-vvikṛtiṁ niśamya Gauḍeśvareṇa bhuvi tasya nareśvaratve Śrī-Vaidyadeva urukīrttir-iyāṁ niyuktaḥ.* ||—v. 13-14.[2]

About this time Anantavarmman *Coḍagaṅga* invaded Western Bengal and overran the country up to the banks of the Ganges:—

> *Gṛhṇāti-sma karaṁ bhūmer-gaṅgā-gotama-gaṅgayoḥ* । *Madhye paśyatsu vīreṣu prauḍhaḥ prauḍha-striyā iva.* v. 22.[3]

Rāmapāladeva conquered Utkala and Kaliṅga during the reign of either Rāja-Rāja I or his son Anantavarmman. It appears that Anantavarmman invaded the territories of the Pāla Kings immediately after the death of Rāmapāla. It may be mentioned in this connection that Vaidyadeva is said to have obtained a naval victory in Southern Bengal, and it is quite possible that this victory was obtained over the naval forces of Anantavarmman:—

War with the King of Orissa.

> *Yasy-ānuttara-vaṅga-saṅgara-jaye nauvāṭa-hīhīrava-trastair-ddik-karibhiś-ca yan-na calitaṁ cen-nāsti tad-gamya-bhūḥ Kiñ-c-otpātukake-nipāta-patana-protsarpitaiḥ śīkarair-ākāśe sthiratā kṛtā yadi bhavet-syān-niṣkalaṅkuḥ śaśī.* v. 11.[4]

---

[1] Mem. A.S.B, Vol. III, p. 51.

[2] Epi Ind., Vol. II., p. 351.

[3] J.A.S.B. 1896, Pt. I, p. 239.

[4] Epi. Ind., Vol. II, p. 351.

Nothing is known about the extent of Kumārapāla's reign or the date of his death. But he does not appear to have reigned more than two or three years. He was succeeded by his infant son Gopāladeva (Gopāla III) III:—

Pratyarthi-pramadā-kadamvaka-śiraḥ-sindūra-lopakrama-krīḍā-paṭala-pāṇir-eṣa suṣuve Gopālam-ūrvvi-bhujaṁ । *Dhātrī-pālana-jṛmbhamāna-mahimā-karpūra-pāṁś-ūtkarair-devaḥ kīrttiṁ-a-yonijaṁ vitanute yaḥ śaiśave krīḍitaṁ.*[1] v. 17.

The infant king seems to have been murdered very soon after his accession:—

Api śatrughnopāyād-gopālaḥ svar-jagāma tatsūnuḥ | *Hantu* (*ḥ*) *kumbhīnasyās-tanayasy-aitasya sāmayikam-etat.*[2] v. 12.

A posthumous record of this king has been discovered by Babu Aksaya Kumāra Maitreya at Manda in the District of Rajshahi and presented to the Indian Museum. The palaeography points to the later part of the 11th and the earlier part of the 12th century as its date. The record is full of mistakes and is untranslatable:—

1. *Oṁ sura-sarid-uru-vīcīḥ sīkarau kunda-gauraur-vviracita parabhāgo vāla ca-*
2. *ndr-āvatansaḥ diśatu sivamajansraṁ* । *śambhu-koṭīra-bhāra kalama-kaṇisa roci-*
3. *rmmaṁjarī piṁjarīsu* ‖ *Śri-mad-Gopāladevas-tridīva muṣarātaḥ svepva-*
4. *-yā tyakta kāsas-tasy-āhaṁ pāda-dhūli-prathita iti nijaṁ nāḥ* . *Vuddhām-asthīta-pre-*
5. *-trājñā-pratijño nisita-sarasavaı Purasenasakṛsāṣṭau nisyajā-dallirā*
6. *jā tridaśapuram-agād-Aiḍadeva kṛtajñaḥ* ‖ *Svataṁ tvato vadhū ya saṅgarāt prāpya*
7. *Candra-kiraṇ-āmalaṁ yasaḥ krīḍati tṛdaśasundarī Dṛso deva-eva Śūbhadeva nanda-*
8. *-naḥ* ‖ *Artha tadanuga-gīta-vilāsaḥ dharmmadhvara-masthara-galavāsaḥ Dāma-śūra sasa-*
9. *-maṁ vāhitaveśaḥ sa yayate Śrī-sāmbhāvakadāsaḥ dagdhā yatra madadbhūtāḥ śara-śa-*
10. *-ndhāna-pūritā yatra Bhāvakadāsena Kṛtā kīrṇṇā virājateḥ* ‖ *Rātokena le-*
11. *khitavya.*

We can recognize only a number of names:—

(1) *Gopāladeva*, (2) *Dāmaśūra*, (3) *Aiḍadeva*, (4) *Subhadeva*, (5) *Purasena*, (6) *Sāmbhāvakadāsa*, (7) *Bhāvakadasa* and (8) *Rātoka*, the scribe.

The murder of the infant king and the subsequent accession of his uncle Madanapāla seems to point to a parallel of the murder of the infant King Edward V by his uncle Richard III. About this time some dispute seems to have arisen about the succession, and ultimately Madanapāla's party seems to have triumphed. Vaidyadeva ignores Madanapāla completely in the Kamauli copper-plate grant issued in the fourth year of his reign, and so it must be admitted that Vaidyadeva declared his independence after the murder of Gopala III. Till the reign of Madanapāla the Pāla Kingdom consisted of Eastern Magadha and Northern Bengal.

His murder by Uadanapāla.

[1] J.A.S.B., 1900, Pt. I, p. 71.

[2] Mem. A.S.B., Vol. III, p. 51.

Taking advantage of the internal dissensions in the Pāla Kingdom, Vijayasena seems to have strengthened himself in Eastern and Western Bengal, and when the weakness of the Pālas under Madanapāla became apparent, he invaded Northern Bengal and succeeded in wresting the southern part of Varendra. Madanapāladeva seems to have continued to hold the northern part of Varendra, as his Manahali Grant was issued in the 8th year of his reign from the royal city of Rāmāvatī.[1]

Conquest of Southern Varendra.

We learn from the Deopārā inscription that Vijayasena attacked the King of Gauḍa with great force :—

Tvaṁ Nānya-Vīra-vijay-īti girah kavīnāṁ śrutvāṣ-nyathā-manana-rūḍha-nigūḍha roṣaḥ : Gauḍendram-adravad-apākṛta Kāmarūpabhūpaṁ Kaliṅgam-api yas-tarasā jigāya. v. 20.[2]

Most probably Madanapāla is the Gauḍendra mentioned in the verse quoted above. It is stated in the Deopārā inscription that Vijayasena defeated and imprisoned the King of Mithilā named Nānyadeva, so most probably Vijayasena conquered the remaining portion of Varendra before he turned his attention towards the neighbouring district of Mithilā. Madanapāla's dominions were confined to the limits of Magadha after this. Vijayasena did not remain content with Varendra. He despatched a flotilla of armed boats for the conquest of the Western regions.

Conquest of Northern Varendra.

Vijayasena invades Magadha.

Pāścātya-cakra-jayakeliṣu yasya yāvad-Gaṁgā-pravāham-anudhāvati nauvitāne Bharggasya mauli-sarid-ambhasi bhasma-paṅka-lagn-ojjhit-eva tarir-indu kalā cakāsti. v. 22.[3]

But the expedition does not seem to have been very successful, as otherwise the incident would surely have been mentioned in Sena inscriptions. Madanpāladeva was greatly assisted in his war against Vijayasena by Candradeva, the founder of the Gahaḍavālā Dynasty of Kanauj. The author of the Rāmacarita has gratefully acknowledged this in his work :—

Siṁhī-suta-vikrānten-arjjuna-dhāmnā bhuvaḥ pradīpena । Kamalā-vikāśa-veṣaja viṣajā Candreṇa vandhunopetām ॥ 20. Caṇḍī-caraṇa-saroja-prasāda-sampanna-vigraha-Śrīkaṁ : Na khalu Madanaṁ s-āṅgeśam-īśāṁ agād jagad-vijayalakṣmīḥ v. 21.[4]

Madanapāla seems to have been defeated by Vijayasena some time after the year 1108 A.D., which is the probable date of his Manahali inscription, when Candradeva was dead. Candradeva must have died before 1104 A.D., as in that year the Basāhi Plates of his grandson Govinda-Candra were issued, and that prince is styled "Mahārājaputra", so it must be admitted that Candradeva had ceased to reign at that time, and his son Madanpāla sat on the throne.[5]

---

[1] J.A.S.B., 1900, Pt. I, p. 93. [2] Epi. Ind., Vol. I, p. 306. [3] Ibid., p. 307. [4] Mem. A.S.B., Vol. III, p. 307. [5] Ind. Ant., Vol. XIV, p. 103.

Nothing is known about Madanapāla save that he continued to reign for about eleven years longer. Nothing is known about his sons or successors, their extent of reigns or dominion. About fifty years after Madanapāla's death, another prince of the Pāla Dynasty seems to have reigned in Magadha, but about this we shall have to speak later on.

Inscriptions.

Four inscriptions of Madanapāla have been discovered up to date, of which three are votive inscriptions, incised on the pedestals of images, while the remaining one is on a copper-plate. The earliest inscription is the "Manahali" Grant, which records the grant of a village, perhaps named Kāṣṭhagiri, in the *Koṭīvarṣa-Visaya* of the *Pauṇḍravardhana Bhukti*, to a Brāhmaṇa named Vaṭeśvarasvāmi-śarmman, an inhabitant of Campāhiṭṭi, as dakṣiṇā for having read the Mahābhārata to the great queen (*Paṭṭa-Mahādevī*) Citramatikā, on the 15th day of the month of Caitra, in the 8th year of the King's reign. The order confirming the grant was issued from the city of Rāmāvatī, which had been founded by Rāmapāla.[1] An image of *Ṣaṣṭhī* dedicated in the same year was discovered by Cunningham on Bihar Hill, but it cannot be traced at present.[2] Another image dedicated on the 30th Āśvina of the 19th year of the King was also discovered by Cunningham at Jayanagar, near Lakhisarai, in the Monghyr District;[3] but this image also is missing at present.

Vijayasena.

After conquering Varendra, Vijayasena founded a new capital on the northern bank of the Ganges and named it after himself. The new capital was situated close to Rāmāvatī and its ruins have recently been discovered by the Varendra Research Society.[4] He built a new temple of Siva named "Pradyumneśvara" on the bank of a large tank, the site of which also has been identified by the Varendra Archæological Society. This temple was situated in the village of Devapārā or Deopārā, which is about six miles distant from Vijaypur Milik, the site of Vijayapur, the capital founded by Vijayasena. Vijaypur Milik itself is situated on the banks of the river Ganges, about ten miles due east from the town of Rampur-Boalia.

His conquest.

After defeating the King of Gauḍa, who has been identified with Madanapāla, Vijayasena attacked Mithilā and conquered several Kings, viz., *Rāghava*, *Vardhana* and *Vīra*.[5] He led an expedition to Kāmarūpa and most probably succeeded in overthrowing Vaidyadeva or his successor.[6] We learn from the Deopara Inscription that he defeated the King of Kaliṅga. Most probably Anantavarmman *Coḍagaṅga* led another raid into Western Bengal, but was repulsed by Vijayasena. Vijayasena's dominions comprised of Eastern Bengal, Western Bengal and Northern Bengal. An unpublished copper-

His Kingdom.

plate grant of this King was issued from the victorious camp at Vikramapura, and so it must be admitted that Eastern

1 J.A.S.B., 1900, Pt. i, p. 71.
2 A.S.R., Vol. III, p. 124, No. 16. Epi. Ind., Vol V. App. p. 87, Note 4.
3 Ibid., p. 125, No. 17, Vol. XV, p. 174; Epi. Ind., Vol. V, App. p. 87, No. 645.
4 Gauḍarājamālā, p. 65.
5 Epi. Ind., Vol. I, p. 309.
6 Ibid.

Bengal formed a part of his kingdom, and also that the Varmman Dynasty had ceased to reign. The kingdom was bounded on the East by that of Nānyadeva in Mithila and that of Madanapāla in Magadha. Vijayasena must have reigned for at least forty years, as his newly-discovered copper-plate grant was issued in the 37th year of his reign. He was succeeded by his son Vallālasena, and the name of his wife Vilāsadevī is known to us both from his own copper-plate grant and that of his son. Only two inscriptions of Vijayasena have been discovered up to date. The most important one is the Deopārā praśasti, recording the erection of the temple of Pradyumneśvara, which must form the basis of all new accounts of the Sena Dynasty, for some years to come. The other inscription is the newly-discovered copper-plate grant, which was brought to me for decipherment by a friend several years ago, but which I am unable to trace at present. This plate records the grant of a village to a Brāhmaṇa of Śāṇḍilya Gotra as the *dakṣiṇā* of the *Tulāpuruṣa ceremony* performed by the Queen Vilāsadevi, and was issued from Vikrampura in the 37th year of the King. Vijayasena's death seems to have taken place about the year 1108 A.D. Vijayasena was succeeded by his son Vallālasenadeva, who seems to have been an aged man when he came to the throne. His name is well known throughout Bengal as the founder of Kulinism. But as neither his own copper-plates nor those of his son Lakṣmaṇasena contain any references to Kulinism, even when referring to Brāhmaṇas to whom land was granted, the legend about its origin should be accepted with great caution. The whole system may be of much later origin and of no historical importance at all. Vallālasena's dates, as found in some works on Law and Astronomy, the authorship of which are ascribed to him, are misleading. These dates are found in some verses in the Dānasāgara, a work on Law, and in the Adbhūtasāgara, a work on Astronomy. I have pointed out elsewhere that these verses are not to be found in all manuscripts of these two works, and should, therefore be taken as later additions.[1] According to these verses, the Dānasāgara was compiled by Vallālasena in S. 1091 = 1169 A.D.[2] and the Adbhūtasāgara was begun by him in S. 1090 = 1168 A.D.[3] Mr. Manomohan Chakravartti has discovered another verse in the Dānasāgara, according to which Vallālasena ascended the throne in S. 1081 = 1159 A.D.[4], but these verses are hardly of an historical importance, as they appear to be later additions. If, on later enquiry, these verses can be found in all the manuscripts discovered, even then they cannot be accepted as basis for the construction of a chronology, so long as they are to be found in modern manuscripts. If they can be found in manuscript records of the 12th and 13th century A.D., then only these dates can be accepted as correct. I have tried to show elsewhere that the Bodh-Gayā inscriptions of Aśokacalla[5] prove that Lakṣmaṇasena died before 1070 A.D.,[6] consequently, unless some contemporary

Length of reign: Successors and relations: Inscriptions.

---

1 J.A.S.B., Vol. IX (New Series), p. 272.

2 Ibid., 1896, Pt. I, p. 23; Eggeling's Catalogue of Sanskrit MSS. in India Office Library, p. 545.

3 Bhandarkar's Report on the Search for Sanskrit MSS. during 1887—88 and 1890—91, p. lxxxv.

4 J.A.S.B. (N. S.), 1906, p. 17, Note.

5 Cunningham's Mahabodhi, p. 78, and Ind. Ant., Vol. X, p. 341.

6 J.A.S.B. (N. S.), Vol. IX, p. 272.

record can be cited as evidence, it cannot be said, on the basis of the verses in the Dān asāgara and the Adbhūtasāgara, that Vallālasena came to the throne in 1159 A.D. and wrote a book on Law ten years later. Only one inscription of this King has been discovered up to date This is a copper-plate grant discovered in January, 1911, at Sītāhāṭi, near Kātwā, in the Burdwan District of Bengal. It records the grant of the village of Vāllahiṭṭa in the Uttara Rāḍhā *Maṇḍala* of the Varddhamāna *bhukti* to a Brāhmaṇa named Ovāsudeva-Śarmman as the *Dakṣiṇā* of the *Hemāśva-Mahādāna* (the gift of a golden horse), performed by the Queen Vilāsadevi, the King's mother, on the 16th Vaiśākha in the 11th year of his reign.[1] The Dūtaka of this grant was the King's minister of peace and war, *Hari-ghoṣa*, who is the only officer of Vallālasena whose name has come down to us. Vallālasena married Rāmadevī of the Calukya family and was succeeded by his son Lakṣmaṇasena. As the initial year of the Laksmanasena era is 1119-20 A.D., so Lakṣmaṇasena must have ascended the throne in that year, consequently, Vallālasena cannot be taken to have reigned more than 12 or 13 years. He seems to have been a peaceably inclined, weak, old man, studious in his habits, and a patron of Brāhmanism. Both he and his father seem to have belonged to the Śaiva sect, as their inscriptions begin with an invocation to Śiva.

Inscription.

Step by step, the Gāhaḍavāla Kings of Kanauj advanced towards the East. Govindacandra seems to have conquered the whole of Magadha in the earlier part of his reign (1114 = 54 A.D.). In 1127 he was in a position to grant a village in the Patna District to a Brāhmaṇa. An unpublished grant, a photograph of which has been kindly lent to me by Prof. Jadunath Sircar, M.A., of the Patna College, records the donation of the village of Pādoli, together with the village of Guṇāve in the Maṇiari *Pattalā*, to a Brāhmaṇa of the Kāśyapa Gotra named Gaṇeśvara-Śarman, after bathing in the Ganges at Kānyakubja, on Sunday, the 11th of the dark half of Jyaiṣṭha of the Vikrama year 1183 = 1127 A.D. I have been given to understand by Prof. Sircar that this new inscription will shortly be published in the Journal of the Asiatic Society of Bengal. The invasion of Magadha by the Gāhaḍavāla King seems to have led to hostilities between Govindacandra and Lakṣmaṇasena. In the Madanapāḍa Grant of Viśvarūpasena and Edilpur Grant of Keśavasena, Lakṣmaṇasena is said to have erected pillars of victory at Benares (*Vārāṇasī*) and at Allahabad (*Triveṇī*).

Gāhaḍavāla Conquest of Magadha.

The Patna Grant of Govindacandra, v.s. 1183.

Belāyāṁ dakṣinavdher-mmūśala-dhara gadāpāṇi saṁvāsavedyāṁ Tīrotsaṅge triveṇyāh kamalabhava-makhārambha nirvvyājapute yen-occair-yajña-yūpaiḥ saha samara-jayastambhamālā nyadhāyi. v.[2]

The Maṇiari *Pattalā* mentioned in the copper-plate grant of Govindacandra mentioned above has been identified with the modern Muner, a village of considerable importance in the Patna District, which was a well-known place in the 12th century. Bakhtiyar Khilji directed some of his expeditions against this town before the

[1] Vaṅgiya Sāhitya Pariṣat Patrikā, Vol. XVII, Pt IV, pp. 237-38.
[2] J.A.S.B., Vol. VII, p. 43, and Vol. 1896, Pt. I, p. 9.

conquest of Bihar and Bengal.[1] Govindacandra advanced as far as Monghyr in the year 1146 A.D. and granted the village of Tatacavāḍa in the Paṇḍalā *Pattalā*, in Govisāloka, that belonged to Dudhāli in Saruvāra, to a Brāhmana named Ṭhakkura Śrīdhara, after bathing in the Ganges at Mudgagiri (Monghyr) on the occasion of the Akṣayatṛtīya, on Monday the 3rd of the bright half of the Vaiśākha of the Vikrama year 1202, the 15th April, 1146 A.D.[2] Govindacandra was most probably leading an expedition into Bengal when he bathed in the Ganges at Monghyr, and granted the village mentioned above. The expedition was no doubt unsuccessful, because, otherwise, the event would surely have been mentioned in some Gahaḍavāla inscription. The use of the era of Lakṣmaṇasena in two inscriptions at Bodh-Gayā[3] prove that in spite of the efforts of the Gahaḍavāla Kings Eastern Magadha continued to be in the possession of the Senas up to 1193 A.D. Most probably the river Son was the boundary line of the Gahaḍavāla and the Sena Kingdoms.

Govindracandra invades Bengal.

Lakṣmaṇasena, the son of Vallālasena, ascended the throne in 1119 A.D. He was an energetic and able ruler like his grandfather Vijayasena. In the lifetime of his father he led an expedition into Kaliṅga.[4] After his accession to the throne he defeated the King of Benares, i.e., Govindacandra, in battle and conquered Kāmarūpa.[5] In the copper-plate grants of his sons, Keśavasena and Viśvarūpasena, he is said to have planted a pillar of victory on the shores of the Southern Ocean, which most probably means that he defeated some Southern King in battle. Nothing is known about his length of reign, but his kingdom consisted of Eastern, Western and Northern Bengal and the eastern part of Magadha. It is also probable that part of Mithilā was included in his kingdom.

Laksmanasena.

Four copper-plate inscriptions and one stone inscription of this king has been discovered up to date. The earliest of these is the Tarpandighi Grant, found in 1874 at Tarpandighi at Gangarampur in the Dinajpur District. It records the grant of the village of Vilvahiṣṭi in the Pauṇḍravardhana *bhūkti* as the dakṣiṇā of the Golden Horse and Chariot ceremonies (*Hemāśva-ratha*) to a Brāhmaṇa named Śrī Iśvara Śarmman.

During the reign of Lakṣmaṇasena the western part of Magadha seems to have passed into the hands of the Gāhaḍavāla Kings of Kanauj. The local rulers practically acquired independence, as an example of which we may cite the name of the Mahānāyaka Pratāpadhavala of Jāpila. The earliest record of this generation is a short rock inscription near the Tutrahi Falls in the Shahabad District, the date of which corresponds to 19th April, 1158 A.D.[6] According to an unpublished inscription at Rohṭasgaḍh, the King set up some monuments on the 27th March, 1169 A.D.[7] In the same district, there is another rock inscription at Tārāchaṇḍi incised in the Vikrama era 1225, corresponding to 1169 A.D. According to another inscription at Rohtaṣgaḍh, the family to which this dynasty belonged is called Khayāravāla *Vaṁśa*

1 Tabakati-i-Nasiri, Trans. by Raverty, p. 550.
2 Epi. Ind., Vol. VII, p. 98.
3 Cunningham's Mahabodhi, p. 78, and Ind. Ant., Vol. X, p. 346.
4 J.A.S.B. (N.S.), Vol. V, p. 467.
5 Ibid.
6 Epi. Ind., Vol. IV, p. 311.
7 Ibid., Vol. V, App. p. 22, No. 152.

The relations between this chief and the Gāhaḍavāla Kings of Kanauj has been made clear by the Tārāchaṇḍī inscription of the same prince. This inscription was edited by Dr. Fitz-Edward Hall in 1860.[1] According to this inscription, in Samvat 1225 on Wednesday, the 3rd day of the dark half of Jyaiṣṭha, = 16th April, 1169 A.D., Pratāpadhavala announces that a certain copper-plate recording the grant of the villages of Kalahaṇḍī and Baḍapilā has been obtained by several Brāhmaṇas by bribing one, Deu, the slave of King Vijayacandra of Kānyakubja. The inscription finally adds that the proprietary share of the rent should be collected yearly as before. This inscription shows very clearly that though Pratāpadhavala was semi-independent, he was obliged to recognize the suzerainty of the Gāhaḍavāla King of Kanauj. The villages stated above within his territories could be granted by the King of Kānyakubja to anybody he liked.

After the death of Lakṣmaṇasena three of his sons seem to have come to the throne:—(1) Mādhavasena, (2) Viśvarūpasena and (3) Keśavasena. Nothing is known about the order of succession of these princes and their dates. Elsewhere I have tried to prove that Mādhavasena precedes the other sons of Lakṣmaṇasena, Viśvarūpa, and he in his turn preceded Keśavasena. One copper-plate inscription of each of these princes have been discovered, viz., those of Viśvarūpa and Keśavasena. A copper-plate of Mādhavasena has been preserved in a monastery in the Tehri State.[2]

Viśvarūpsena is known from his now lost Madanapāḍa Grant[3] of the year 14 of his reign. It records the grant of certain lands in the village Piñjakāṣṭhī in the Vikramapura division (*bhāga*) of Eastern Bengal (*Vaṅga*) of the Pauṇḍravarddhana *bhukti* to a Brāhmaṇa named Viśvarūpadeva-śarmman. His brother Keśavasena is also known from his Edilpur Grant[4] of the year 3, which records the grant of certain lands in the province (*pradeśa*) of Eastern Bengal, the division (*bhāga*) of Vikramapura and the *bhukti* of Pauṇḍravarddhana to Īśvaradeva-Śarmman, a brother of the Visvarūpadeva Śarmman of the Madanapāḍa Grant. The Sena Dynasty came to an end with the Muhammadan occupation of East Bengal, and the last kings are not known.

The Fall of the Senas.

In 1161 A.D. we find a king named Govindapāladeva in Magadha. His existence is proved from a stone inscription and six manuscript records. But we are not yet in a position to state clearly whether he belonged to the Imperial Pāla Dynasty or not. Yet the affix Pāla and the Buddhist titles (e.g. *Parama-saugata*) would lead us to believe that he was descended from them. He seems to have come to the throne in 1161 A.D.,[5] as the Gayā Stone Inscription distinctly mentions that his fourteenth regnal year fell in V.S. 1232 = 1175 A.D. A manuscript of the *Aṣṭasāhasrikā Prajñāpāramitā* discovered by Hodgson at Nepal, which was copied in the fourth year of the King's reign, mentions the

Govindapāla.

[1] Journal of the American Oriental Society, Vol. VI, p. 547.
[2] Atkinson's Kumayun.
[3] J.A.S.B., 1896, Pt. I, p. 6, pl. I & II.
[4] J.A.S.B., Vol. VII, p. 43.
[5] Cunningham's Arch. Survey Report Vol, III., p. 124.

name of Nālanda (?) as the place of copying.[1] So it may be assumed with a tolerable degree of certainty that Govindapāla ruled a portion, probably the eastern one, of Magadha. The records which mention this king contain some curious phrases and will be edited before we come to discuss the events of the king's reign :—

1. THE GAYA STONE INSCRIPTION OF GOVINDAPĀLA.

This record was found in the walls of a small shrine to the south of the main shrine of Gadādhara, just below the courtyard of the Viṣṇupad Temple at Gayā It has already been mentioned by Cunningham,[2] who reproduced it in a lithograph, and by Kielhorn.[3] It is incised on the back-slab of an image of a female deity with four hands and consists of fifteen horizontal and one vertical lines. A *lingaṁ* is to be found at the top of the record, which runs as follows :—

1. *Oṁ*[4] *oṁ svasti namo bhagavate Vāsudevaya . Vrahmaṇo dvitīya parārdhe* ।
2. *Vārāha-kalpe vaivaśvata manvantare Aṣṭāviṁśatime yuge kalau pūrvvasaṁ-*
3. *-ndhyāyāṁ saṁvat* 1232 *Vikāri saṁmvatsare Śrī Govindapāla-de-*
4. *-va-gatarājye caturddaśa saṁmvatsare Gayāyāṁ* ॥ *Vaśiṣṭha-gotro-*
5. *-ti-guṇo dvivedaḥ Śrī Ḍallaṇo* [s] *sūta-sūtaṁ mahāntaṁ* । *Vidyādharaṁ gu*
6. *gulinaṁ Gadābhṛn-maṭhe anākāri dhanā dvijānāṁ* ॥ *bhokṣāthaṁ-avdaṁ pra-*
7. *ti-ṣoḍaś-aiva kārṣāpaṇī vṛddhita-eva ladhvāḥ Mūlañ-ca* । *pañcāsad-i*
8. *-h-āsti sākṣī Padm-ābhidhāno-tha ca Viśvarūpa* ॥ *Nṛsiṁha Śrī-dharodeva*
9. *Dharo Śrī* (?) *daṇḍa* (?) *nā(ya)kau* । *Viṣṇu-seva-karau c-aite tapovana-nivāsinaḥ* ॥ *Rāghavaḥ*
10. *Śrīkaro s Sūko Dāmodarakaḥ Hīdharau Bhikhodeva nidhirddharmmī c-aite pāla-*
11. *-na-kāriṇaḥ* । *A-candrārkam-imaṁ dharmmaṁ pālayiṣyanti ye sukhaṁ* । *pratyavdaṁ te-*
12. *-śvamedhasya phalaṁ prāpsanti mānavāḥ* ॥ *Āśvine śukla-pañcamyāṁ bhojyaṁ yo*
13. *vārayed-idaṁ* । *Labhate sāv-asaṁligdhaṁ mahāpātaka-pañcakaṁ* । *praśasti-*
14. *-r-iyaṁ kṛtā Śrī-Yuktendreṇa likhitā c-eyaṁ Kājasīyī-Jaya-kumārābhyāṁ* ॥
15. *Oṁ*[5] *Someśvaro-tra sākṣasti Padmanābho Gayādvija Devarūpasya purato dattā c-aite Kaparddakā* । .

The only peculiarity noticeable in this inscription is the use of the word *gate*. The words giving the regnal year may be taken—

(1) to mean that the *Vikāri Saṁvatsara* and V.S. 1232 fell in the 15th regnal year, i.e. when the 14th was expired;

(2) to mean that Govindapāla himself was dead, but this was the 14th year from the date of his consecration;

---

[1] R. L. Mitra, *Aṣṭasāhasrikā Prajñāpāramitā* (Bib. Ind.), p. xxii Note: but see also the Catalogue of the Hodgson MSS. in the Royal Asiatic Society's Collection—J.R.A.S. (N.S.), Vol. VIII, p. 3.

[2] Cunningham's Arch. Survey Report, Vol. III, p. 125, pl. XXXVIII, No. 18.

[3] Epi. Ind., Vol. V, App. p. 24, No. 166.

[4] Expressed by a symbol.

[5] On right side.

(3) to mean that Govindapāla was alive, but that part of the country which once belonged to him, had *then* ceased to do so.

At the time of the Muhammadan conquest, we find similar peculiar wording in inscriptions and colophones of MSS. The second conclusion is obviously wrong, as we know from the colophone of one of the Sanskrit MSS. in the Cambridge University Library (see No. 5 below) that his kingdom was destroyed (*Vinaṣṭa*) in his 38th regnal year; so he could not have died before that date. The first interpretation is also obviously impossible, as there is no evidence in the whole range of Northern India Inscriptions of an "expired regnal year" being used to express a date. The third explanation is the only one applicable to the particular case. We find a parallel case in the Belkhara Inscription of V.S. 1253 [1]

The rest of the records are colophones of manuscripts.

(2) Colophone of a MS. of the *Aṣṭa-sāhasrikā Prajñāpāramitā* (last page only) recently acquired by Mahāmahopādhyāya Hara Prasāda Śāstrī:—

1. *—vāpya ca dhārayitvā vācayitvā—vāpya pravarttānāṁ viharantu sadārthina iti* ‖ *Ye dharmmā hetu prabhavā*
2. *(he)tun-teṣān-tathāgato hy-avadat-'eṣāñ-ca yo nirodha evaṁ vādī mahāśram-aṇaḥ* ‖ *Deyadharmoyaṁ pravara-mahā-yāna (yāyi-)*
3. *naḥ Khānodakīya Yaśarāpur-āvasthānevaṁ* ‖ *Dānapati Kṣānti-rakṣitasya yadatra puṇyan-tadbhavaty-ācary-opādhyāya mā*
4. *tā pitṛ pūrvaṁgamaṁ kṛtvā sakala satva-rāśer-anuttara-jñāna-phal-āvāptaya iti . Śrīmad-Govindapāladevasy-ātīta*
5. *Samvatsa* 18 *Kārttika dine* 15 *Caṅgaḍa pāṭakāvasthita Khānodakīya Yaśar-āpure Ācarya Prajñānu—*

(3) Colophone of a MS. of *Amarakoṣa* in the collection of the Asiatic Society of Bengal:—

1. *-ṣepi tat* ‖ *Arthāntāḥ ādy-alaṁ prāpt-āpanna-pūrvvāḥ paropagāḥ* । *taddhitārthe dviguḥ saṁkhyā-sarvvaṇāma-tad-antakāḥ* ‖ *Vahuvrīhir-adig-nāmnām-un-neyaṁ tad-udā-*
2. *-hṛtam* ; *Guṇa-dravya-kriyā-yog-opādhibhiḥ* (portion of the palm-leaf torn out) *r-agāminaḥ* । *Kutaḥ karttaryasaṁjñāyāṁ kṛtyāḥ karttari karmmaṇi* , *Anādy-ant-āstena rakt-ādy-arthen-ā*
3. *-nartha-bhedakāḥ* । *Pada-sañjñakāmiṣu yuṣmad-asmat-tiṅavyayaṁ* ‖ *Paraṁ virodhi śeṣam tu jñeyaṁ śiṣṭa prayogataḥ* ‖ *Liṅgasaṅgrahaḥ samāptaḥ* ,
4. *Paramabhaṭṭārak-ety-ādi rājāvalī pūrvvavat Śrī-Govinda-pālīya saṁvat* 24 *Caitra śudi* 8 *śubham-astu sarvva jagatām-iti* [2]

(4) Colophone of a MS. of the *Guhyāvalī vivṛiti* in the collection of the University of Cambridge [3]:—

1. *Yad-alambhi puṇyan-ten-āstu sarvva-jagataḥ kila bodhi-lakṣmīḥ* । *Yat sarvva-satva-janit-āśubha-yogatohaṁ syān-nārak-ānala-vṛto*

---

[1] J.A.S.B (N.S.), Vol. VII, p. 757. [2] J.A.S.B., 1900, Pt. I, p. 100, no. 25.

[3] Bendall's Catalogue of Buddhist Sanskrit MSS. in the University Library, Cambridge, p. 188.

2. *-nalinī-suhamsaḥ* ‖ *Guhy-āvalī-vivṛtiḥ* ‖ *Vivṛtiḥ paṇḍita-sthavira-Śrī-Ghanade-vasya* ‖

3. *Govindapāladevānāṁ saṁ* 37 *Śrāmaṇa dine* 11 *likhitam-idaṁ pustakaṁ kā Śrī-Gayākareṇ-eti* ‖

(5) Colophone of a MS. of the *Pañcākāra* in the collection of the University of Cambridge:—

1. *Hemante Ratnasambhavaḥ* । *Vasante Amitābhaḥ* । *Grīṣme Amogha-siddhiḥ* । *Śiśire Vajrasattvaḥ* । *Dharmma-dhātu Vajrasatvaḥ dvāre Vajrasa-*
2. *-tvaḥ* । *Sarvva-trailokyam-ekākāra-vajrasatvaḥ praśasyate* । *pañcākār-ātmakaṁ sarvvaṁ trailokyaṁ sacarācaraṁ* । *yady-api rājyaṁ nirvvika-*
3. *-lpamayaṁ dṛśyate* । *Jagat pañcaskandha-svabhāvena pañca-Vuddhāḥ pra-kīrttitāḥ* । *Pañcāvaraṇa-nirmmuktā Vuddhāḥ syuḥ pañca-*
4. *Kaulikāḥ* । *Kāni pañc-āvaraṇāni jñeyāni kleśas-tathā janma-karmma-saṁjñ-ānam-ajñānañ-ca tath-aiva-ca* । *pañcāvaraṇāni*
5. *c-aitāni kathitāni tathāgataiḥ* । *Evaṁ vimṛṣyamāṇo bhāvayet satataṁ prāp-ṇotyagrajāṁ vodhim* । *Samyak-sambuddha-bhāṣitaḥ pañcākā-*
6. *-raḥ samāptaḥ* ‖ *Parameśvar-ety-ādi rājāvalī pūrvvavat* । *Śrīmad-Govinda-pāla-devānāṁ vinaṣṭa-rājye aṣṭa-triṁśat-samvatsare s*
7. *bhilikhyamāne* । *Jyaiṣṭha-Kṛṣṇ-āṣṭmyāṁ tithau Yatra saṁ* 38 *Jyaiṣṭhadine* 8 *likhitam-idaṁ pustakaṁ Kā Śrī-Gayākareṇ-eti*

(6) Colophone of a MS. of the *Yoga-ratna-mālā* by Kāhṇa or *Kṛṣṇācārya* in the collection of the University of Cambridge[1]:—

1. *-de* । *Mahāsūkṣma-savāg-gocaratvāt* । *Vajrastathāgatāḥ* । *Teṣāmmaṇḍaṁ sāraṁ.* । *Nabho-ghanam-anābhāṣatvāt* । *Virajaskaṁ kleśakṣayāt Mokṣadaṁ*
2. *Saṁsārātikrāntavāt* । *Pitā te tvam-as-īti* । *Tath-aiva praty-ātma-vedytvāt* । *Vajrapadmayor-adhiṣṭhānaṁ yen-ādhiṣṭhyate* । *Yogaratnasya mālā*
3. *-yāṁ kṛtvā Hevajra-pañjikām* । *yat-puṇyam-ācitaṁ tena nikleśaḥ syād-akhilo janaḥ* ‖ *Śrī-Hevajrapañjikā Yogaratnamālā sa-*
4. *-māptā* ‖ *Kṛtir-iyaṁ Paṇḍit-ācārya Śrī-Kahṇa-pādānām-iti* । *Parameśvar-ety-ādi rājāvalī pūrvvavat* । *Śrīma-*
5. *-dgovindapāladevānāṁ saṁ* 39 *bhādradine* 14 *likhitam-idaṁ pustakaṁ kā Śrī Gayākareṇa* ‖

(7) A MS. of the *Aṣṭasāhasrikā Prajñāpāramitā* examined by Mahāmahopādhyāya Hara Prasāda Śāstrī in 1893. "The work is on palm-leaves pressed between two wooden boards, with sticks inserted through holes in place of strings. One of the boards is besmeared with sandal paste, which has accumulated there for ages. The MS. was evidently an object of worship, and as Prajñāpāramitā is also called Rakshā-Bhagavatī, it appears to have been regarded as a charm for protection against evils. The MS. was copied in the 38th year of Govindapāla, who is styled Gauṛeśvara, i.e. the year 1198 A.D.[2]

---

[1] Bendall's Catalogue of Buddhist Sanskrit MSS. in the University Library, Cambridge, p 190.

[2] J.A.S.B., 1893, Pt. I, p. 253.

(8) A MS. of the Prajñāpāramitā of 8000 verses in the collection of the Royal Asiatic Society of Great Britain and Ireland written at Nālanda in the fourth year of the King's reign :—

1. *Mātā-pitṛ-pūrvaṁgamaṁ kṛtvā sakala-satva-rāśer-anuttara-jñāna-phal-āvāptaya iti* ‖ *Parameśvara Paramabhaṭṭāraka Paramasaugata Mahārājādhirāja Śrī-mad-Govindapālasya-vijaya-rājya-saṁvatsare* 4 *Śūny-odaka-grāma-vāstavya Śri-man-Nālanda-*
2. *m-astu sarva-jagatām.*[1]

It will be observed that out of these eight records only two mention the King as living. In No. 8 we find the usual titles and no peculiarity, consequently it can be admitted that Govindapāla reigned for at least four years. In No. 4 though titles have been omitted yet the absence of such formulæ as "*Parameśvaretyādi Rājāvalī-pūrvvavat*" at the beginning, and such phrases as "*gatarājye*," "*atītarājye*" and "*vinaṣṭa-rājye*" make it certain that the King Govindapāla was alive in the 37th year from the date of his consecration, i.e. 1197 A.D. This being admitted, we find that the phrases *gata* and *atīta* are used in other records in a peculiar sense, signifying that the reign of the Prince was at an end, in that particular locality, but that it was still continuing at some other place. Thus in the Gayā Inscription of the Vikrama year 1232 the use of the word gata means that Govindapāla's reign had ceased at Gayā, but was continuing somewhere else. The use of the word *Atīta* in the MS. discovered by Mahāmahopādhyāya Hara Prasāda Śāstri, which was copied in 38th year of his reign, signifies that his reign was at an end at the place where the MS. was copied. Only the use of the special word *Vinaṣṭa* in No. 6 signifies that the remnants of his authority was destroyed in that year, as has been correctly interpreted by Bendall,[2] by the Muhammdans under Bakhtyār-Khilji. It appears that Govindapāla ruled lower part of Eastern Magadha close to Nālanda and yet bore the title of *Gauḍeśvara*. He was recognized as the real King by Buddhists in all parts of the country. He managed to continue his reign till 1199, when Cauhān, Gahaṛwāṛ, Pāla and Sena were all swept away by the whirlwind of Muhammadan invasion.

Extent of Kingdom.

Postscript.

An inscription of the time of Vigrahapāla III was found by me recently on the pedestal of an image of Buddha in the Indian Museum. This appears to be the inscription mentioned by Cunningham.[3] It runs as follows :—

1. *Śri-mad-Vigrahapāla-deva-rājya samvat* 13 *mārgga dine* 14.
2. *Deya* [*dha*] *rmmoyaṁ suvarṇṇakāra Dehekasya Sāhe sutasya* ‖

"The year 13, the 14th day of Mārggaśirṣa, of the reign of the illustrious Vīgrahapāladeva. The religious gift of the goldsmith Deheka, son of Sāhe."

1 J.R.A.S. (N.S.), Vol. VIII (1876), p. 3; Astasbasrika-Prajnaparamita (Bib. Ind., Calcutta, 1888), Preface, p. xxii, Note.

2 Catalogue of Buddhist Sanskrit MSS. in the University Library, Cambridge, Introduction, p. iii.

3 A.S.R., Vol. III, p. 121, no. 7.

I have since been informed by Pandit Rajani Kanta Chakravartti of Maldah and Babu Aksaya Kumar Maitreya of Rajshahi that Babu Haridas Palit's identification of Amarti with Ramanti is not correct. I am also informed that there are no villages called Jagdalā or Ḍamrol near Amarti in the Maldah District.

R. D. BANERJI.
20 7-1914.

of the Asiatic Society of Bengal.

Vol. I.

I. *On certain Tibetan Scrolls and Images lately brought from Gyantse.—By* PROF. SATIS CHANDRA VIDYABHUṢAṆA, M.A., M.R.A.S. (Price Re. 1-8; or 2*s.* 3*d.*)

II. *Sal-Ammoniac: a Study in Primitive Chemistry.—By* H. E. STAPLETON, B.A., B.Sc. (Price Re. 1; or 1*s.* 6*d.*)

III. *The Similarity of the Tibetan to the Kashgar-Brahmi Alphabet.—By* The REV. A. H. FRANCKE. (Price Rs. 2; or 2*s.* 10*d.*)

IV. *Alchemical Equipment in the Eleventh Century, A.D.—By* H. E. STAPLETON and R. F. AZO. (Price Re. 1-8; or 2*s.* 3*d.*)

V. *Malaysian Barnacles in the Indian Museum, with a list of the Indian Pedunculata.—By* N. ANNANDALE, B.A., D.Sc. (Price Re. 1-8; or 2*s.* 3*d.*)

VI. *Ashrafpur Copper-plate Grants of Devakhaḍga.—By* GANGA MOHAN LASKAR, M.A. (Price Annas 8; or 10*d.*)

VII. *Festivals and Folklore of Gilgit.—By* GHULAM MUHAMMAD. (Price Rs. 2; or 2*s.* 10*d.*)

VIII. *Notes on the Bhotias of Almora and British Garhwal.—By* C. A. SHERRING, M.A. F.R.G.S., I.C.S. (Price Re. 1-5; or 2*s.*)

IX. *Religion and Customs of the Uraons.—By* the late REV. FATHER DEHON, S.J. (Price Rs. 2; or 2*s.* 10*d.*)

X. *Notes on the Fauna of a Desert Tract in Southern India* (Herpetology and Entomology).—*By* N. ANNANDALE, D.Sc., C.M.Z.S., with a list of Mammals by R. C. WROUGHTON, F.E.S. (Price Rs. 2; or 2*s.* 10*d.*)

XI. *Amulets as Agents in the Prevention of Disease in Bengal.*—Compiled in the Office of the Superintendent of Ethnography, Bengal. (Price Annas 12; or 1*s.* 2*d.*)

XII. *Earth-Eating and the Earth-Eating Habit in India.—By* D. HOOPER and H. H. MANN. (Price Re. 1; or 1*s.* 6*d.*)

XIII. *On a Cup-Mark Inscription in the Chumbi Valley.—By* E. H. C. WALSH, I.C.S. (Price Re. 1; or 1*s.* 6*d.*)

XIV. *A Descriptive List of the Sea-Snakes* (Hydrophiidæ) *in the Indian Museum, Calcutta.—By* CAPTAIN F. WALL, I.M.S., C.M.Z.S. (Price Re. 1; or 1*s.* 6*d.*)

XV. *Common Saws and Proverbs collected, chiefly from Dervishes, in Southern Persia.—By* LIEUT.-COL. D. C. PHILLOTT. (Price Re. 1; or 1*s.* 6*d.*)

XVI. *The Common Hydra of Bengal: its Systematic Position and Life History.—By* N. ANNANDALE, B.A., D.Sc., C.M.Z.S. (Price Re. 1; or 1*s.* 6*d.*)

XVII. *Animals in the Inscriptions of Piyadasi.—By* MONMOHAN CHAKRAVARTI, M.A. (Price Annas 12; or 1*s.* 2*d.*)

XVIII. *Some current Persian Tales told by Professional Story-Tellers.—By* LIEUT.-COL. D. C. PHILLOTT. (Price Re. 1; or 1*s.* 6*d.*)

XIX. *The Dards at Khalatse in Western Tibet.—By* REV. A. H. FRANCKE. (Price Re. 1-6; or 2*s.*)

Supplement, Miscellanea Ethnographica. Part I. 1. *The Blow-Gun in Southern India* 2. *Miscellaneous objects from the Râmanâd subdivision of the Madura district* 3. *Indian Weighing-beams.—By* N. ANNANDALE, D.Sc. (Price Re. 1.)

Supplement, Miscellanea Ethnographica. Part II. 1. *Some Malayan Weapons—By* N. ANNANDALE. 2. *Plan of a Persian Gentleman's House.—By* LIEUT.-COL. D. C. PHILLOTT. (Price Annas 8; or 10*d.*)

Memoirs of the Asiatic Society of

Vol. II.

I. *Cirrhipèdes operculés de l'Indian Museum de Calcutta.—Par* M. A. GRUVEL. (Price Rs. 2; or 2s. 10d.)

II. *The Coinage of Tibet.—By* E. H. C. WALSH. (Price Re. 1; or 1s. 6d.).

III. *The Exact Determination of the Fastness of the more Common Indigenous Dyes of Bengal, and comparison with typical synthetic Dye-stuffs. Part I. Dyeing on Cotton.—By* E. R. WATSON. (Price Re. 1; or 1s. 6d.)

IV. *The Saorias of the Rajmahal Hills.—By* R. B. BAINBRIDGE. (Price Rs. 2; or 2s. 10d.)

V. *Mundari Poetry, Music and Dances.—By* REV. FR. J. HOFFMANN, S.J. (Price Re. 1; or 1s. 6d.)

VI. *Tarikh-i-Nuṣratjangi.—By* HARINATH DE. (Price Re. 1; or 1s. 6d.)

VII. *The Exact Determination of the Fastness of the more Common Indigenous Dyes of Bengal, and comparison with typical Synthetic Dye-stuffs. Part II. Dyeing on Silk.—By* E. R. WATSON. (Price Annas 12; or 1s. 2d.)

VIII. *Monograph on Sea Snakes.—By* MAJOR F. WALL, I.M.S. (Price Rs. 5; or 7s.)

IX. *A Polyglot List of Birds in Turki, Manchu and Chinese.—By* E. DENISON ROSS, PH.D. (Price Rs. 4; or 6s.)

X. *Notes on some Monuments in Afghanistan.—By* H. H. HAYDEN. (Price Re. 1; or 1s. 6d.)

XI. *On the Correlations of Areas of Matured Crops and the Rainfall, and certain allied problems in Agriculture and Meteorology.—By* S. M. JACOB, I.C.S. (Price Rs. 2-8; or 3s. 10d.)

Vol. III.

I. *Ramacarita by Sandhyakara Nandi.—Edited by* MAHAMAHOPADHYAYA HARAPRASAD SHASTRI, M.A. (Price Rs. 2; or 2s. 10d.)

II. *An Alchemical Compilation of the 13th Century A.D.—By* H. E. STAPLETON, B.A., B.Sc., *and* R. F. AZO. (Price Re. 1; or 1s. 6d.)

III. *The Journals of Major James Rennell, F.R.S., First Surveyor-General of India.—Edited by* T. H. D. LATOUCHE. (Price Rs. 4; or 6s.)

IV. *Lisu Tribes of Burma-China Frontier.—By* A. ROSE *and* J. COGGIN BROWN. (Price Rs. 3; or 4s.)

V. *The Vyavahâra-Mâtrikâ of Jimutavāhana.—By* THE HON. JUSTICE SIR ASUTOSH MOOKERJEE, SARASWATI, KT., C.S.I., M.A., D.L., D.SC., F.R.A.S., F.R.S.E. (Price Re. 1-8; or 2s. 3d.)

VI. *Some Current Pushtu Folk Stories.—By* F. H. MALYON, *21st Punjabis.* (Price Re. 1-8; or 2s. 3d.)

VII. *The Chank Bangle Industry.—By* J. HORNELL. (Price Rs. 2; or 2s. 8d.)

VIII. *Catuhśatikā by Arya Deva.—By* MAHAMAHOPADHYAYA HARAPRASAD SHASTRI, C.I.E. (Price Rs. 2; or 2s. 10d.)

IX. *Father A. Monserrate's Mongolicae Legationis Commentarius.—By* REV. H. HOSTEN, S.J. (Price Rs. 4; or 5s. 4d.)

Vol. IV.

(In the course of publication concurrently with V.)

I. *Sanskrit-Tibetan-English Vocabulary: being an edition and translation of the Mahāvyutpatti by* ALEXANDER CSOMA DE KÖRÖS.—*Edited by* E. DENISON ROSS, C.I.E., PH.D., F.A.S.B., *and* MAHAMAHOPADHYAYA SATIS CHANDRA VIDYABHUSANA, M.A., PH.D., F.A.S.B. Part I. (Price Rs. 5; or 7s.)

II. Ditto ditto Part II. (In press.)

Vol. V.

I. *Srid-pa-ho—a Tibeto-Chinese Tortoise Chart of Divination.—By* MAHĀMAHOPĀDHYĀYA DR. SATIS CHANDRA VIDYABHUSANA, M.A., PH.D., F.A.S.B. (Price As. 8; or 10d.)

II. *Fragments of a Buddhist work in the ancient Aryan language of Chinese Turkistan.—Edited by* STEN KONOW. (Price Re. 1-8; or 2s. 3d.)

III. *The Pālas of Bengal.—By* R. D. BANERJI. (Price Rs. 5; or 7s.)

Extra No. *Abors and Galongs.—By* GEORGE D-S-DUNBAR. (Price Rs. 6; or 8s. 6d.)

MEMOIRS

OF THE

ASIATIC SOCIETY OF BENGAL

VOL. V, No. 3. Plates XXIV—XXXII, XXXVI—XXXVIII.

PLATES TO ILLUSTRATE

THE PĀLAS OF BENGAL.

BY

R. D. BANERJI, M.A., *Indian Museum, Calcutta.*

CALCUTTA:
PRINTED AT THE BAPTIST MISSION PRESS, AND PUBLISHED BY
THE ASIATIC SOCIETY, 1, PARK STREET.
1915.

Price Rs. 5 or 7s., for text and plates.

4-12-15.

The Visnupad Inscription of Nārāyaṇapāla.—The year 7.

The Krishna-Dwarika temple inscription of Nayapāla.—The year 15.

The Narasiṁha temple inscription of Nayapāla.—The year 15.

The Akṣay Vaṭa Inscription of Vigrahapāla III.—The year 5.

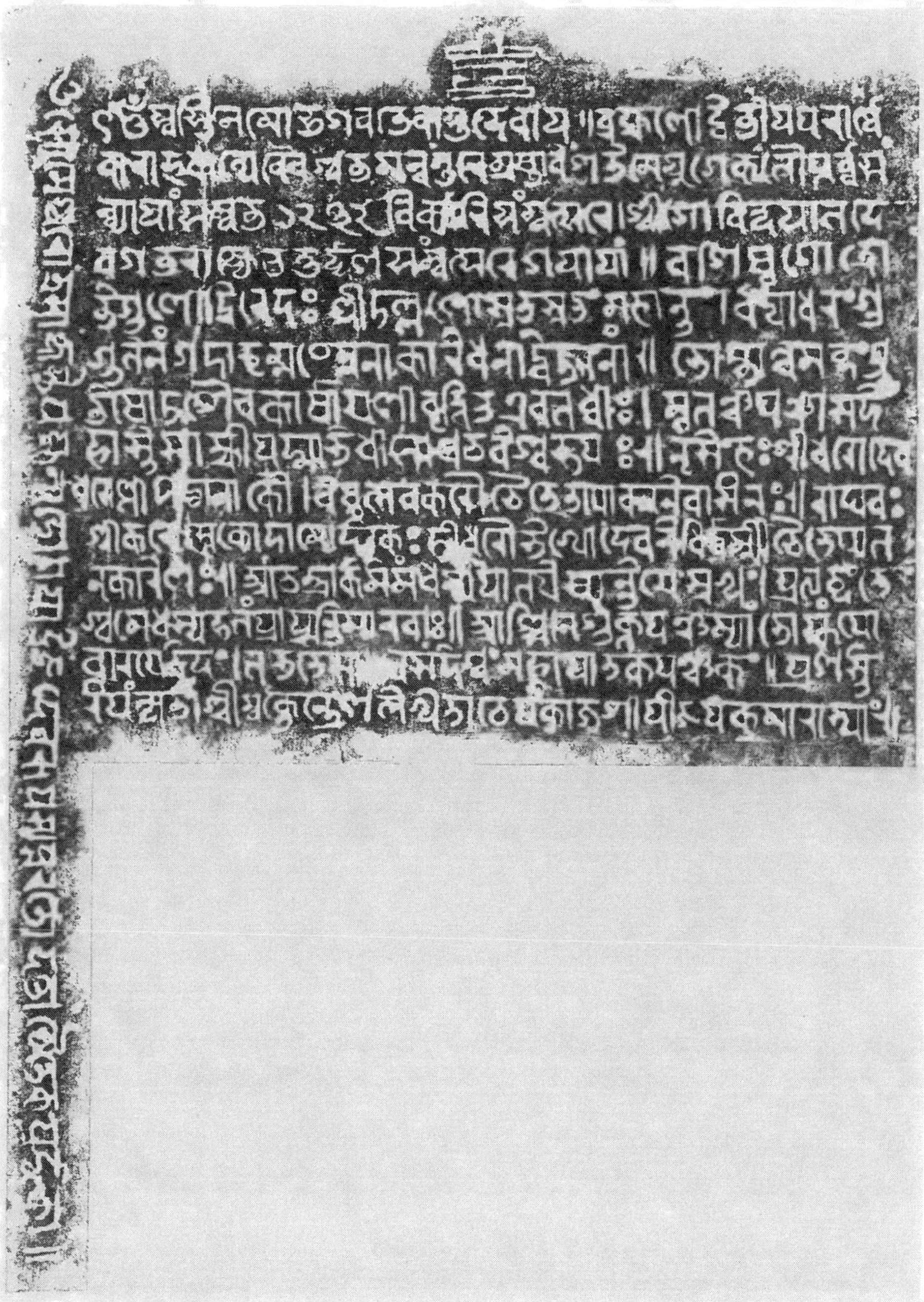

The Vāsudeva temple inscription of Govindapāla.—Samvat 1232.

The Śītalā ghat inscription of Yakṣapāla.

Chandimau (now Indian Museum) image inscription of the 42nd year of Rāmapāla.

Indian Museum image inscription of the 13th year of Vigrahapāla III.

The Manda Inscription of Gopāla III.

Bodh-Gayā image inscription of the 11th year of Mahīpāla I.

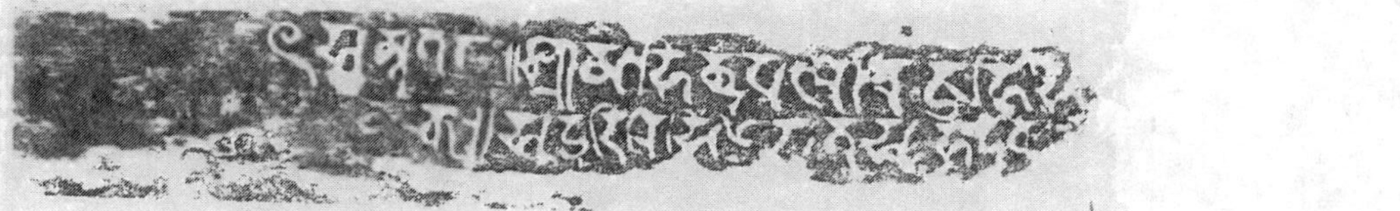

The Ramgaya image inscription of Mahendrapāla.—The year 8.

The British Museum image inscription of Mahendrapāla.—The year 9.

The Vasudeva temple inscription.

The Indian Museum image inscription of Nārāyaṇapāla.—The year 9.

Colophon of Prajñāpāramitā in the Bodleian Libra

Colophon of Prajñāpāramitā. Collection of the Royal Asia

Colophon of Prajñāpāramitā. A.S.B. Collectio

Colophon of Prajñāpāramitā. Private Collection.

amitā in the Bodleian Library. 15th year of Rāmapāla.

Collection of the Royal Asiatic Society. 4th year of Govindapāla.

āramitā. A.S.B. Collection. 6th year of Mahīpāla I.

amitā. Private Collection. 19th year of Harivarmman.

PLATE XXXII.

The Bodh-Gayā Inscription of Jayaccandra.—Samvat 124x.

Colophon of Aṣṭasāhasrīkā Prajñāpāramitā. Copied in the 5th year of Mahīpāla I.
MS. Add. 1464.

Colophon of Amarakoṣa. Collection of the Asiatic Society of Bengal. Copied in the 14th year of Govindapāla.

Colophon of Aṣṭa-sāhasrikā Prajñāpāramitā. Collection of the Asiatic Society of Bengal. Copied in 18th year of Govindapāla.

Colophon of Pañcarakṣā. Cambridge University Library. Copied in the 14th year of Nayapāla. MS. Add. 1688.

Colophon of Aṣṭasāhasrikā Prajñāpāramitā. Copied in the 5th year of Mahīpāla I.
MS. Add. 1464.

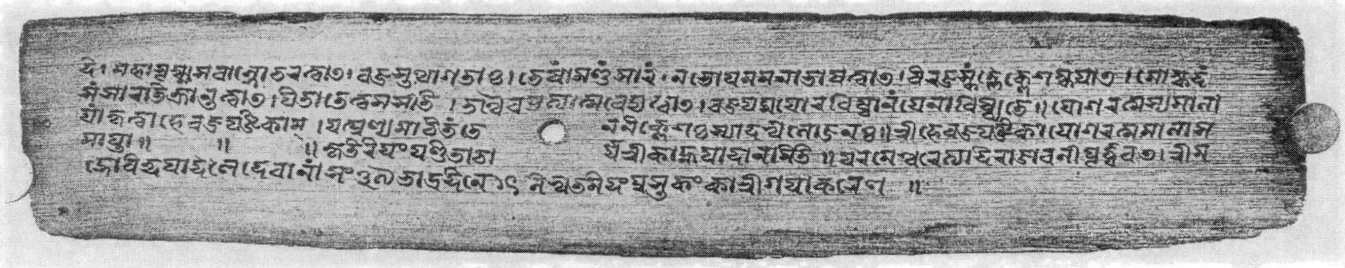

Colophon of Yogaratnamālā. Cambridge University Library. Year 39 of Govindapāla.

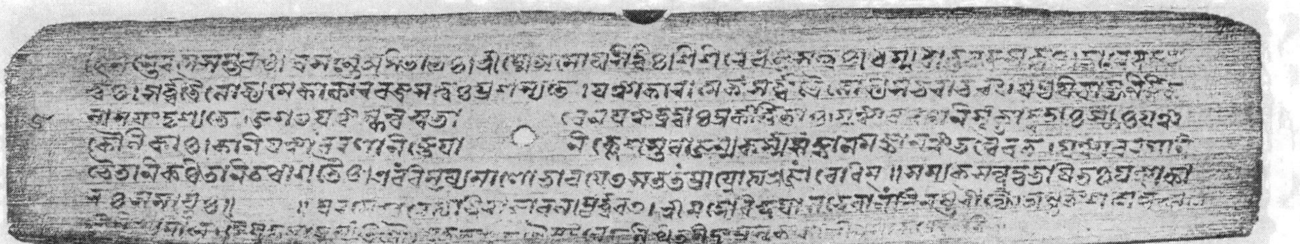

Colophon of Pañcākāra. Cambridge University Library. Year 38 of Govindapāla.

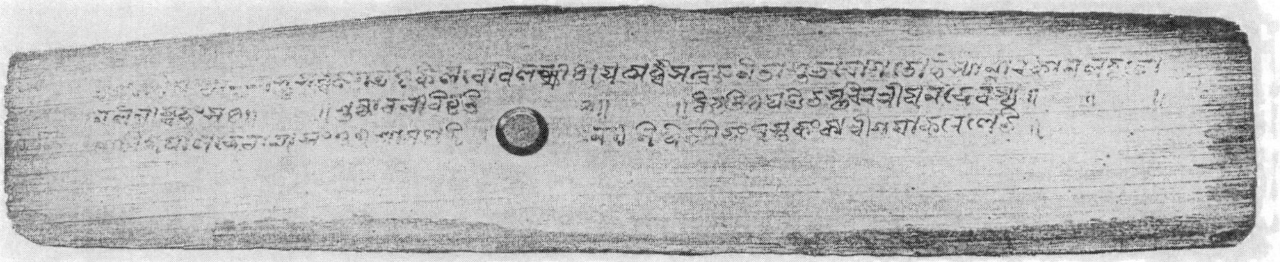

Colophon of Guhyāvalīvivṛti. Cambridge University Library. Year 37 of Govindapāla.

THE PĀLAS OF BENGAL.

By R. D. BANERJI, M.A., *Indian Museum, Calcutta.*

INDEX.

INDEX.

INDEX.

INDEX.

Memoirs of the Asiatic Society of Bengal.

Vol. I.

I. *On certain Tibetan Scrolls and Images lately brought from Gyantse.—By* PROF. SATIS CHANDRA VIDYABHUṢAṆA, M.A., M.R.A.S. (Price Re. 1-8; or 2*s.* 3*d.*)

II. *Sal-Ammoniac: a Study in Primitive Chemistry.—By* H. E. STAPLETON, B.A., B.Sc. (Price Re. 1; or 1*s.* 6*d.*)

III. *The Similarity of the Tibetan to the Kashgar-Brahmi Alphabet.—By* The REV. A. H. FRANCKE. (Price Rs. 2; or 2*s.* 10*d.*)

IV. *Alchemical Equipment in the Eleventh Century, A.D.—By* H. E. STAPLETON and R. F. AZO. (Price Re. 1-8; or 2*s.* 3*d.*)

V. *Malaysian Barnacles in the Indian Museum, with a list of the Indian Pedunculata.—By* N. ANNANDALE, B.A., D.Sc. (Price Re. 1-8; or 2*s.* 3*d.*)

VI. *Ashrafpur Copper-plate Grants of Devakhadga.—By* GANGA MOHAN LASKAR, M.A. (Price Annas 8; or 10*d.*)

VII. *Festivals and Folklore of Gilgit.—By* GHULAM MUHAMMAD. (Price Rs. 2; or 2*s.* 10*d.*)

VIII. *Notes on the Bhotias of Almora and British Garhwal.—By* C. A. SHERRING, M.A. F.R.G.S., I.C.S. (Price Re. 1-5; or 2*s.*)

IX. *Religion and Customs of the Uraons.—By* the late REV. FATHER DEHON, S.J. (Price Rs. 2; or 2*s.* 10*d.*)

X. *Notes on the Fauna of a Desert Tract in Southern India* (Herpetology and Entomology).—*By* N. ANNANDALE, D.Sc., C.M.Z.S., with a list of Mammals by R. C. WROUGHTON, F.E.S. (Price Rs. 2; or 2*s.* 10*d.*)

XI. *Amulets as Agents in the Prevention of Disease in Bengal.*—Compiled in the Office of the Superintendent of Ethnography, Bengal. (Price Annas 12; or 1*s.* 2*d.*)

XII. *Earth-Eating and the Earth-Eating Habit in India.—By* D. HOOPER and H. H. MANN. (Price Re. 1; or 1*s.* 6*d.*)

XIII. *On a Cup-Mark Inscription in the Chumbi Valley.—By* E. H. C. WALSH, I.C.S. (Price Re. 1; or 1*s.* 6*d.*)

XIV. *A Descriptive List of the Sea-Snakes* (Hydrophiidæ) *in the Indian Museum, Calcutta.—By* CAPTAIN F. WALL, I.M.S., C.M.Z.S. (Price Re. 1; or 1*s.* 6*d.*)

XV. *Common Saws and Proverbs collected, chiefly from Dervishes, in Southern Persia.—By* LIEUT.-COL. D. C. PHILLOTT. (Price Re. 1; or 1*s.* 6*d.*)

XVI. *The Common Hydra of Bengal: its Systematic Position and Life History.—By* N. ANNANDALE, B.A., D.Sc., C.M.Z.S. (Price Re. 1; or 1*s.* 6*d.*)

XVII. *Animals in the Inscriptions of Piyadasi.—By* MONMOHAN CHAKRAVARTI, M.A. (Price Annas 12; or 1*s.* 2*d.*)

XVIII. *Some current Persian Tales told by Professional Story-Tellers.—By* LIEUT.-COL. D. C. PHILLOTT. (Price Re. 1; or 1*s.* 6*d.*)

XIX. *The Dards at Khalatse in Western Tibet.—By* REV. A. H. FRANCKE. (Price Re. 1-6; or 2*s.*)

Supplement, Miscellanea Ethnographica. Part I. 1. *The Blow-Gun in Southern India* 2. *Miscellaneous objects from the Rámanád subdivision of the Madura district* 3. *Indian Weighing-beams.—By* N. ANNANDALE, D.Sc. (Price Re. 1.)

Supplement, Miscellanea Ethnographica. Part II. 1. *Some Malayan Weapons—By* N. ANNANDALE. 2. *Plan of a Persian Gentleman's House.—By* LIEUT.-COL. D. C. PHILLOTT. (Price Annas 8; or 10*d.*)

Memoirs of the Asiatic Society of Bengal.

Vol. II.

I. *Cirrhipèdes operculés de l'Indian Museum de Calcutta.—Par* M. A. GRUVEL. (Price Rs. 2; or 2*s.* 10*d.*)
II. *The Coinage of Tibet.—By* E. H. C. WALSH. (Price Re. 1; or 1*s.* 6*d.*).
III. *The Exact Determination of the Fastness of the more Common Indigenous Dyes of Bengal, and comparison with typical synthetic Dye-stuffs. Part I. Dyeing on Cotton.—By* E. R. WATSON. (Price Re. 1; or 1*s.* 6*d.*)
IV. *The Saorias of the Rajmahal Hills.—By* R. B. BAINBRIDGE. (Price Rs. 2; or 2*s.* 10*d.*)
V. *Mundari Poetry, Music and Dances.—By* REV. FR. J. HOFFMANN, S.J. (Price Re. 1; or 1*s.* 6*d.*)
VI. *Tarikh-i-Nuṣratjangi.—By* HARINATH DE. (Price Re. 1; or 1*s.* 6*d.*)
VII. *The Exact Determination of the Fastness of the more Common Indigenous Dyes of Bengal, and comparison with typical Synthetic Dye-stuffs. Part II. Dyeing on Silk.—By* E. R. WATSON. (Price Annas 12; or 1*s.* 2*d.*)
VIII. *Monograph on Sea Snakes.—By* MAJOR F. WALL, I.M.S. (Price Rs. 5; or 7*s.*)
IX. *A Polyglot List of Birds in Turki, Manchu and Chinese.—By* E. DENISON ROSS, PH.D. (Price Rs. 4; or 6*s.*)
X. *Notes on some Monuments in Afghanistan.—By* H. H. HAYDEN. (Price Re. 1; or 1*s.* 6*d.*)
XI. *On the Correlations of Areas of Matured Crops and the Rainfall, and certain allied problems in Agriculture and Meteorology.—By* S. M. JACOB, I.C.S. (Price Rs. 2-8; or 3*s.* 10*d.*)

Vol. III.

I. *Ramacarita by Sandhyakara Nandi.—Edited by* MAHAMAHOPADHYAYA HARAPRASAD SHASTRI, M.A. (Price Rs. 2; or 2*s.* 10*d.*)
II. *An Alchemical Compilation of the 13th Century A.D.—By* H. E. STAPLETON, B.A., B.SC., *and* R. F. AZO. (Price Re. 1; or 1*s.* 6*d.*)
III. *The Journals of Major James Rennell, F.R.S., First Surveyor-General of India.—Edited by* T. H. D. LATOUCHE. (Price Rs. 4; or 6*s.*)
IV. *Lisu Tribes of Burma-China Frontier.—By* A. ROSE *and* J. COGGIN BROWN. (Price Rs. 3; or 4*s.*)
V. *The Vyavahâra-Mâtrikâ of Jimutavāhana.—By* THE HON. JUSTICE SIR ASUTOSH MOOKERJEE, SARAŚWATI, KT., C.S.I., M.A., D.L., D.SC., F.R.A.S., F.R.S.E. (Price Re. 1-8; or 2*s.* 3*d.*)
VI. *Some Current Pushtu Folk Stories.—By* F. H. MALYON, 21*st Punjabis.* (Price Re. 1-8; or 2*s.* 3*d.*)
VII. *The Chank Bangle Industry.—By* J. HORNELL. (Price Rs. 2; or 2*s.* 8*d.*)
VIII. *Catuḥśatikā by Arya Deva.—By* MAHAMAHOPADHYAYA HARAPRASAD SHASTRI, C.I.E. (Price Rs. 2; or 2*s.* 10*d.*)
IX. *Father A. Monserrate's Mongolicae Legationis Commentarius.—By* REV. H. HOSTEN, S.J. (Price Rs. 4; or 5*s.* 4*d.*)

Vol. IV.

(In the course of publication concurrently with V.)

I. *Sanskrit-Tibetan-English Vocabulary: being an edition and translation of the Mahāvyutpatti by* ALEXANDER CSOMA DE KÖRÖS.—*Edited by* E. DENISON ROSS, C.I.E., PH.D., F.A.S.B., *and* MAHAMAHOPADHYAYA SATIS CHANDRA VIDYABHUSANA, M.A., PH.D., F.A.S.B. Part I. (Price Rs. 5; or 7*s.*)
II. Ditto ditto Part II. (In press.)

Vol. V.

I. *Srid-pa-ho—a Tibeto-Chinese Tortoise Chart of Divination.—By* MAHĀMAHOPĀDHYĀYA DR. SATIS CHANDRA VIDYABHUSANA, M.A., PH.D., F.A.S.B. (Price As. 8; or 10*d.*)
II. *Fragments of a Buddhist work in the ancient Aryan language of Chinese Turkistan.—Edited by* STEN KONOW. (Price Re. 1-8; or 2*s.* 3*d.*)
III. *The Pālas of Bengal.—By* R. D. BANERJI. (Price Rs. 5; or 7*s.*)
Extra No. *Abors and Galongs.—By* GEORGE D-S-DUNBAR. (Price Rs. 6; or 8*s.* 6*d.*)
IV. *Mirza Zu-l-Qarnain. A Christian Grandee of three Great Moghuls. With Notes on Akbar's Christian Wife and the Indian Bourbons.—By* REV. H. HOSTEN, S.J. (In press.)